DAVID J. CHAPMAN

The Darkest Path

The Paranormal and Our Layered Reality

Copyright © 2019 by David J. Chapman

All rights reserved. No part of this publication may be reproduced, stored or transmitted in any form or by any means, electronic, mechanical, photocopying, recording, scanning, or otherwise without written permission from the publisher. It is illegal to copy this book, post it to a website, or distribute it by any other means without permission.

David J. Chapman asserts the moral right to be identified as the author of this work.

David J. Chapman has no responsibility for the persistence or accuracy of URLs for external or third-party Internet Websites referred to in this publication and does not guarantee that any content on such Websites is, or will remain, accurate or appropriate.

Designations used by companies to distinguish their products are often claimed as trademarks. All brand names and product names used in this book and on its cover are trade names, service marks, trademarks and registered trademarks of their respective owners. The publishers and the book are not associated with any product or vendor mentioned in this book. None of the companies referenced within the book have endorsed the book.

First edition

Cover art by Alasdair Acott
Editing by ACB

This book was professionally typeset on Reedsy.
Find out more at reedsy.com

Contents

My Father's Death	1
Things Start to Get Weird	5
The Reality of All This	8
Reaching the Point of Total Despair, Reflecting on My...	16
The Descent into Fan Bay and a New Perception of Reality	23
Eastry Hospital Hauntings	30
Samhain 2009	42
We Enter into The Belly of The Beast	45
The Revelation	52
The Night Visitor	55
3rd November 2009, 3 am on the Dot!	61
A Desperate Plea for Help	66
The Radio Show	72
Holiday Hauntings	76
Lilith	78
Our Mother	94
Sadly You are in Need of Training. HM Borstal 1981	106
You're a Stowe Boy Now	111
Time for Your Discharge Beating	113
Did I Learn My Lesson?	116
The Story of Albert's Ghost	120
My Mother's Death	123
A Ghostwriter for a Ghost Story, the Pathway Conspiracy, and...	129
Back to the Bastion, 2018	134
Another Chance, Another Ghostwriter	136

The Quest for Knowledge Goes On	137
Epilogue	142
Dedications	145
Special Thanks	146
Further information	149
About the Author	150

1

My Father's Death

On April 18th 2007, late in the afternoon, my father died. Bernard William Chapman passed, at home, surrounded by members of his family. Present were my mother, myself, my wife, my sister Jane, my niece Lisa, and Lisa's son.

My father had suffered from emphysema for a quarter of a century. Any complication on top of his illness could develop into a major problem. This happened during the two weeks before his death, when he contracted pneumonia. He endured two spells in Intensive Care at the Kent and Canterbury Hospital. For the first week, after his discharge, he began to feel he might recover. The hope was short-lived, the pneumonia proving to be too much for him.

I felt so sorry for him, as he worsened during the period before his death, his suffering clear to us all. Most people would not nd it unusual for a son to feel deep sympathy and pain at the sight of his father's demise. My father was an angry, domineering, monster. Now I saw him cry for the first time. I felt only pity for this once selfish and cruel man. My siblings and I looked at him, a beast who had ruled our home with an iron fist and we felt a need to forgive his past wrongs, to move on.

In his defence, he had changed completely in his later years. He'd shown surprising gentleness taking care of our mother. She, a once strong and proud woman now struggling with Alzheimer's and unable to care for herself. During the final years of his life he, despite constantly gasping for breath, kept the home going. His sudden, unexpected, change, came at a pivotal moment in the story I tell here.

During the months before his death, I learned a great deal about my father.

His doctors had no choice but to tell him the facts as they were; nothing could be done to extend his life. He accepted this in his own way and we decided to bring him home for the time he had left.

We set to work converting our dining room into a makeshift bedroom. My wife and her brother added an oxygen machine, hospital-style bed and other equipment. As soon as it was in place we got him out of the hospital and brought him home to care for him as best we could. It was was April 17th and my father was exhausted after his hospital stay. But he was so happy to be home and as soon as we got him comfortable he asked for a cup of tea, drank it and fell asleep. The next morning, as my wife was getting ready to leave for work he woke and asked for more tea. He was at home and comfortable in his surroundings, unaware that this was his last morning.

I need to add an important point here. A few days earlier my father asked me to make him a promise. He made me give my word I would heal the rift 15 years of war between myself and my older brother had caused. I could only hope that Michael would also be willing to try. This resulted in a disturbingly bizarre supernatural twist.

Later that morning I came downstairs and asked my father how he was. He said he'd had a lovely sleep and would like another cup of tea and, maybe some toast. Even as he spoke I knew something was wrong. He appeared unmoored from his surroundings and the passage of time. He fell asleep again.

My poor mother was having to witness her husband slowly slipping away. The steady advance of her Alzheimer's wasn't enough to rob her of her senses. She kept asking if Bernard was going to die. Us, her adult children stood around, unable to reply. What gently way could we tell her? I was about to try when the nurses from the hospice arrived to check on his condition. Once satisfied he was as comfortable as possible, they spoke to our mother for us. Yes, Bernard was going to die, they said, but everybody was doing what they could to ease his suffering.

The nurses inserted a device that administered a cocktail of drugs to make his last few hours easier. As the drugs took effect my father's shoulders dropped, his body relaxing. "Is that any better?" I asked. He sighed a contented sigh and said, "oh yes".

Those were the last legible words he ever spoke.

Or were they?

Soon after the paranormal roller coaster ride began. A ride which prompted me to start writing, attempting to piece it all together.

2

Things Start to Get Weird

Standing next to my father as he died, I felt something rush past me. It was bizarre and unnerving, was this my father's soul leaving his body? Do others experience things like that when present at the death of another human being? I can say it happened to me, but can't explain it, nor make sense of it. Maybe others who have experienced it could do a better job.

Professional people came, and my father went out of the front door for the last time. A deep gloom descended on us. The events of this darkest of days broke my mum. Jane, my sister, stayed with her all night, the rest of us settled down to try and sleep. As we were drifting off, Alison, my wife, remembered that the windows in the dining room were still wide open. She sighed, clearly in no mood to trek back downstairs. Even so, she swung her legs out of the bed, went out onto the landing, then down the stairs. Moments later she was back, her feet having pounded back up the stairs. She was in a state of some distress.

"Christ, Alison, what's happened?" I said.

She shook as she spoke. As she'd reached across the now-empty hospital bed to close the curtains, she'd heard a whispered voice.

It was my father's voice.

I looked at her as if she were mad, which caused her to yell "My God! Your dad spoke to me!"

"Don't be so daft", I replied.

She insisted she had heard him. "Well, what did he say?" I asked, humouring her.

"It was 'good night', or 'goodbye', but it sounded distorted, like out of a broken radio, so I can't be sure"

I looked at her, thinking she must be overtired, imagining things. But she was sure, and soon I was sure. She had heard what she had heard; my father, distorted by distance or time or god knows what, speaking to her.

It sounded ridiculous, the kind of thing you see on TV, or hear on those radio stations with lots of adverts, but it had happened to my wife. I had no reason to doubt her, no reason to think she was lying. The more I considered the event, the surer of an afterlife I became, though I have no desire to preach here.

The thought of him being still 'present' in some form was comforting, if disturbing. But later on, things became creepy and weird, for me, for my family, even for my usually sceptical brother.

Then it was a smell of toast all over the house. First, it appeared when my mother went into the kitchen to make a cup of tea. A smell of toast filled the room, hot, buttered toast. Naturally enough I assumed she was making it, and I called through to her.

"Are you making, toast, mum?"

"No" she shouted back, "would you like me to?"

I said nothing.

Over the following months, the toast smell became common. It spread out across the family, fanning out from our house to the houses of my brother and sisters. Soon we all smelled toast.

3

The Reality of All This

I spent the weeks after my father's death devastated by grief. I hadn't expected it to have been such an ordeal, to have hit me so hard. Why should I care? What made me feel this way? He'd been a constant figure of fear during my childhood, terrorising his children. Why was I now inconsolable? Perhaps, in a way I hadn't realised, I had loved him. Hostages often identify with their captors, the phenomenon known as Stockholm Syndrome. Was I experiencing a form of that?

I spent the next few weeks in deep soul searching, trying to reach the root of my dreadful feeling of regret. What cut deepest was the sense I'd missed a chance to make things right, that the opportunity to understand this man had been lost to me. I knew I hadn't felt anything before he died, why then was I overwhelmed by the love that poured out towards my father? I wasn't alone, my siblings likewise expressed an affection I'd never known them share.

It was in this state of mind that I picked the song for his funeral. 'The Living Years' by Mike and the Mechanics felt like it had been written for us. We all missed my father, we all related to the line 'we all talk a different language, talking in defence'. Arranging the funeral kept me busy and focused, but I was still shocked at how soon the day arrived.

I arrived early and found one of the undertakers. I had my diving watch and the notion I should have him buried wearing it had gnawed away at me until I had to act. They were happy to oblige, placing it on his left wrist. I had known one of the pallbearers when I was young, and he'd been a bit of a rogue. After I was satisfied the watch was firmly in place, I turned to him and said: "I'll be going to the grave with a metal detector to make sure you don't nick it!"

He laughed, not sure if he should take me seriously or not. The Funeral Director stepped in, "Sir will be able to hear it ticking", his words helping to dissipate some of the sadness I felt welling up.

I had no way of knowing how that joke would come back to haunt me, and others.

The funeral was exactly as I wanted it to be. Like me, my father loved the sea, and he'd told my mother he wished he'd seen me scuba diving, hence the watch. Alongside the watch I wanted his RAF service recognised. The RAF ensign was draped over the coffin and his coffin was saluted as the Last Post played. It was a beautiful moment, something he would have loved, and I was proud to have been able to give him such a send-off.

With the funeral over and my father buried, all that remained were his clothes and effects. For the sake of my mum, we kept them as he'd left them, for several years. I continued to feel a deep despair for months afterwards.

At half-past midnight the following night, a scream woke my household. My sister was back staying with us, supporting my mother. We had all gone to bed a couple of hours earlier, emotionally and physically drained, but now here she was, wide awake, running up the stairs. She burst into my mother's room and threw herself onto the bed. My poor mother, shocked awake by the scream and only half awake, looked baffled. My sister calmed herself, "I heard dad trying to speak to me! The bed in the dining room moved, as if someone was getting out of it, then I heard an 'errhhh' sound, right by my ear. I shit myself and ran up here hell for leather!" She looked around at us, I glanced at my wife, was this the same voice she'd heard on the night my father died? When my sister said the voice was distorted, impossible to understand, we knew it was.

Three weeks later something happened, something odd, yet something that didn't register right away. I was in pain from a shattered leg, the result of a bike accident. This, combined with the loss of my father and falling out with my brother Michael, had caused me to sink into deep misery. Doctors were telling me I might lose my leg! I kept asking what the odds were, they kept telling me it was fifty fifty, what kind of bedside manner was that?

I sat in our living room, sick, in pain, my blood swimming with the antibiotics I was forced to take. They stopped the wounds around the pins in my leg becoming infected but I paid the price. I slumped on the sofa, my misery consuming every part of my reality, barely registering mum and Alison. Zoned out, sick both in body and soul, I was jerked into awareness by a sudden sound. A very loud electronic alarm, right next to my left ear. It went on for at least five seconds, maybe even ten.

"What the hell was that?" I asked, looking from mum to Alison and back again.

"What was what?" asked mum, glancing up from her magazine.

"The alarm! The loud alarm!"

Alison looked at me, "What alarm?"

What alarm? How could they not have heard it? It was piercing, shrill almost, and so loud I would have been able to hear it upstairs!

I jumped off the sofa, regretting it almost immediately as pain shot up my leg and sudden nausea caused my head to swim. I swayed for a moment then began looking on the shelves, in the drawers, in the cupboards, searching for the source of the alarm. There was nothing there! No matter where I looked I couldn't find the source of the alarm.

I dropped back onto the sofa. Was the TV on? Yes, it had been on the whole time, perhaps I'd heard that? I told myself that was the only explanation, albeit one that did nothing to explain why I only heard it in my left ear. I shrugged, it must have been nothing. I forgot about it.

Three days later, my older brother Michael came to see us for the rst time in more than fifteen years. It was uncomfortable for both of us, only a handful of years earlier we'd have happily killed each other. Worse, neither of us would have lost a moment's sleep if we had. The bad blood between us went all the way back to our childhood, back to birth even. We hated each other, a deep painful hatred that burned down the years without any sign of ever cooling. Now we were face to face, trying to bridge the canyon between us. Dad had told us to, his last words demanded we at least try.

The conversation was stilted, agonisingly forced. A mixture of small talk and attempts to discuss the past were coming to nothing. I would try to bring up a shared memory, Michael would shoot it down. He'd try to instigate a game of cricket, or sea diving, and I'd clam up. It was horrible and we could tell we'd wasted our time.

Then Michael flinched. He was no longer listening to my halting attempt at asking him about his car. "What's that noise?" he asked, looking to his left, then over his shoulder.
  "What noise?" I asked
  "It's like an electric alarm, like a beeper, or something, it's fucking annoying!"
  I couldn't hear anything, but I was sure I knew what he was hearing.
  "Is it right next to your left ear?" I asked, my excitement growing.
  "Yes!"
  A cold chill ran down my spine. Michael was hearing the sound I'd dismissed as my imagination or the TV. Now I knew it was real, now I knew I hadn't imagined it.

I thought of the watch, buried with my father, firmly clasped to his left wrist. I had purchased the watch second hand because I needed a diver's watch as part of my scuba diving equipment. It was a good one and there was no way I would have been able to afford to get it new. The only problem I'd ever had was down to the lack of a manual, and the alarm I was unable to switch off. Every day, day in day out, my watch alarm would beep loudly. Why the previous owner had set it to go off at midday was a mystery, but I learned to live with it as it was such a good watch and ideal for my diving. But it had driven Alison mad when I first got it, and we'd spent many hours trying to turn that alarm off.

"What time is it?" I asked Alison.

"A couple of minutes after twelve," she replied.

Jesus, my brother and I had heard my watch! But how could that be? It was impossible! The watch was buried with dad! How could we be hearing it here? Mum and Michael had known nothing of the watch, Michael had no reason to make it up.

I had no answers to the questions now swirling around my head. I felt as if the walls of my reality were crumbling away as if everything I'd ever learned was false.

I can't imagine anyone else in my situation would have the faintest clue what to expect next. Even so, I had no way of knowing these events were only the tip of the iceberg. Events were to become ever more shocking over the following months. In fact, they were so astonishing they changed my perception of reality forever. My life was wrenched onto a new path, and my outlook on the supernatural forever shifted. I learned that 'ordinary' people didn't necessarily live 'ordinary' lives.

I cannot pretend the events hadn't left the family fearful. We were desperate for answers to explain what had happened, what it all meant. Speaking for myself, I became obsessed with the supernatural, my thirst for understanding growing daily. The intensity of my need for answers never dulled and even now I still grasp for answers. Some of them I think I've found, some remain stubbornly elusive. Whatever the findings of my investigations, I have kept on digging.

Eventually the watch alarm stopped, but not before it was heard many times more. The weird thing was it wasn't limited to my home; Christine, my sister, heard it a year or two later in her house. Then my brother heard it at his home, many many miles away. How could that happen?

It was only when we hadn't heard it for a while that we realised it had left us, the absence drawing our attention. Weeks of silence turned to months, then years. Had my father left us alone, or had the battery in the watch finally run down?

Though time passed, and (at least on the surface) things appeared to settle down, weird things still happened. I believe my late brother, Robin, visited us late one December day. It was a nondescript afternoon, one of those where the world seems to have breathed out a long, bored, sigh. The afternoon had resigned itself to the only thing on TV being repeats of Only Fools and Horses, and was preparing a disinterested slouch into evening. Suddenly there was the smell of Benylin cough medicine. Not a slight odour either. No, it was so bad I wondered if there was a broken bottle nearby.

I hated that smell! It caught in the back of my throat, trying to draw out a dry retch. I had to find it. I searched the house, each room in turn. Where was it coming from, that sickening sourness? At every cupboard door I told myself it would be in here, a sticky brown mess and broken glass, but there was nothing.

Then I realised. Robin. It was Robin.

Robin the drug addict, Robin the abuser of any substance he could get his hands on. Robin, dead since 2007. Fucking Robin! His fix of choice had been Benylin, easily obtainable and able to get him high. He stank of it, that same cloying stench that now filled the house. I remembered how it had been when he'd visit, the smell so overwhelming it'd take three full days to clear.

Sure enough, after three days the Benylin smell abruptly vanished.

On one of the many days I spent laid up on the couch, my shattered leg slowly knitting back together, he returned. I couldn't get up easily, couldn't move around without a great deal of effort, so would lie on the sofa watching the TV. Homes Under The Hammer was coming to an end, I'd barely watched it to be honest, the pain drawing my focus away from the screen, when I saw someone. Out of the corner of my eye a head and shoulders peered around the kitchen door. Only one person had ever done that, Robin. He'd never felt the need to be polite and knock at the front of the house, he'd always gone around the back and let himself in. He'd open the kitchen door and lean out to see who was in the living room.

I turned my head to get a clearer look, but whoever it was had gone. The house was locked, I was alone. Of course I doubted myself, of course I pulled myself up to my feet and (in great pain) made a circuit of the house, calling to anyone there. There was no-one, and I was certain Robin had visited again.

4

Reaching the Point of Total Despair, Reflecting on My Four-Year Ordeal Trying to Make Sense of it all

The passing years did nothing to reduce the pain in my leg. My surgeon tried his best, always attempting to be positive when I was in the depths of despair. But I was still on crutches, frustrated and wondering if the rest of my life would be this shape. I had twelve operations, not a single one succeeding in getting me back on my feet. I ended up in an Ilizarov Frame, a device resembling a medieval torture device in look and feel. I was at the end of my rope, my soul flaking away with each day that passed.

When my right tibia came apart, leaving me screaming in pain, I finally called out to God, demanding answers. I lay in the bed, agony flaying at my mind and body, waiting for the paramedics and cursed Heaven with all the strength I had.

Was this all there was? Was this all the human condition comprised of: pain, misery, suffering, followed by a pathetic and even painful death? Was this all I was? A hollowed out, broken man, reliant on metal and plastic and painkillers simply to exist? My dark mood swamped me, I saw no future, drew no solace from even the happiest of my memories. I hovered in a dark cloud of anguish, wondering if I had enough Morphine to kill myself.

I had, and I nearly used it more than once.

I don't consider myself religious, but at times like those who doesn't cling to any foolish hope? I was frustrated, in pain, angry. I wanted a magic wand waved by God to fix my leg. "Come on! Fix me!" I glared at the ceiling, daring the mighty deity to relieve my pain and suffering.

Nothing, fucking nothing. No lightning bolt, no clash of thunder, not even a reassuring voice in the dark. If God was listening he chose to ramp up the pain, undo the healing over and over. I was in utter despair, convinced I would never walk again. I gave up fighting.

Now at rock bottom, caught between the equally unsavoury options of a life of pain, or suicide I considered a third way: Amputation. It seemed drastic, but no less awful than any other path I could take. I contacted my doctor, Professor Marsh, and demanded my right leg be removed below the knee. Bound by his oath 'First Do No Harm' he was vehemently against the idea, but I insisted. I was adamant the leg had to go.

"You don't have to live with it!" I'd said, my voice almost reaching a shout, "You don't have to look at this fucking mess, feel the pain all the time!" I paused, surprised to feel a tear in my eye. My voice now quieter, I continued "Professor, you've got to help me, I can't go on like this… please, please help"

He paused, a long drawn out moment I was certain would end in another refusal. He looked down at my file, open on his desk, sighed, looked up at me, "Are you sure you want this,

David? This can never be undone if you go ahead with it…"

I cut him off before he could go on, "Yes, I'm sure, it's time."

I was referred to the Douglas Bader unit at Roehampton. It took a month to see the surgeon who would do the operation. He was a kind man yet still urged me to reconsider. I told him I was sure what I wanted, told him I had a clear mind and was aware of the ramifications. He agreed and sent me back to Stanmore for a last appointment with Professor Marsh, before my transfer to Roehampton.

Three weeks later I arrived at the X-Ray department at Stanmore. I was to have my leg imaged before seeing my doctor. I had sat for X-Rays so many times by then I'm amazed I didn't glow! They could have held a photography exhibition with the amount of pictures they had of my mangled leg. Once again I had the standard images taken, so far nothing was unusual. It was when they asked me to come back in for some more X-Rays that I began to wonder if something was up.

Sent back to the waiting room, I saw a lot of people coming and going from Professor Marsh's consulting room. Marsh was in there with Peter Calder, another surgeon I knew. Craning my neck a little to get a better view I saw they were both looking at my X-Rays, and talking animatedly, occasionally glancing out to me. I waved to them, feeling a little foolish. They looked at me again, then Marsh walked to his door and opened it fully, "You might as well come in David, considering we're discussing you."

In the room, Professor Marsh couldn't hide his smile. "David, you remember how your last X-Ray showed a total non-union? That the bone had failed to heal and we were considering another osteotomy?"

I nodded, I'd not wanted to go through what was essentially

having the bone ends whacked with a hammer and chisel to make them bleed!

He continued, "Well, today's photos tell a rather different story, your tibial fracture is healing!"

I looked from him to Doctor Calder, who nodded and smiled. "Seriously?" I asked.

"Yes, David, it's healing very rapidly, to be honest, we're a little bit surprised!"

Had my prayers been answered? Certainly, my leg was doing something it shouldn't, but was it supernatural? I thought back over the events of the previous years, the incident around the death of my father and the suffering I'd endured since.

I'd gone through such an awful time, even facing people from my past who relished the opportunity to attack me in my weakened state. I'd been physically attacked more than once, and the verbal abuse had been horrific. Could that be coming to an end? Could I allow myself to believe the years of wires and kevlar rings holding my leg together could end? And that would mean an end to the antibiotics! Antibiotics which had me shitting and puking all the time.

I'd endured so much pain, faced so much indifference and outright incompetence in my treatment. Now it was looking as if an end was near! I had to remind myself that not all people are awful, not all futures hopeless. I felt a light of anticipation ignite within me, a newly minted desire for healing.

At least you'd think I'd have felt that. In reality the miraculous healing of my shattered limb did nothing to improve my spirits. I was depressed, my mental health a clouded fog of constant misery. Had the loss of two family members and the fall-out from my accident enacted a heavier cost than I'd realised? Whatever was causing my malaise, I no longer cared if I lived or died.

Around this time I remembered a promise I'd made to myself. Bedridden, miserable, unable to consider a future, I had tried to distract myself with the internet. My idle browsing had led me to a site about urban exploration, specifically wartime bunkers and tunnels in Kent. I had told myself I would visit the locations mentioned if I ever walked again. Now I was healing.

I began contacting the people who'd made the videos, firing messages off in the hope they'd be seen and replied to. The replies were sparse and those who did respond were clear they would not share location information. Maybe they did this to protect me, many of the location, abandoned by the Ministry of Defence, had fallen into disrepair.

They were also secretive, more so than I would have expected from simple urban explorers. Given the events of the previous months and years, I considered the real chance they might be up to no good in these out-of-the-way locations. Where better to do things you don't want to be seen than in places where no eyes look?

I was frustrated. All I wanted to do was follow through on the promise I'd made to myself! How hard could it be? Could I find them myself? I had a vague idea of the locations, so I scoured Google Earth for any landmarks matching what I could see in the videos. I knew I would likely fail in my endeavour: most of the entrances to such places were tiny, small hatches hidden by years of growth.

When I matched up enough detail of one location to be confident I'd find it I was amazed. My efforts had paid off! I'd pinned down the entrance to the Old Fan Bay Deep Shelter to within a few meters!

My leg feeling stronger by the day, I hopped in my four-wheel drive and hit the road to Dover. I parked near the cliffs and continued on foot. How wonderful to be walking! Could it really have been I was considering giving up my leg so recently? It was raining heavily, yet I strode on, determined to succeed. I filled my lungs with the sea air, the sound of gulls wheeling overhead while the distant boom of the sea rumbled almost inaudibly.

I was overly optimistic about the state of my leg. Though it was, undeniably, healing I was soon weakening. The wind and rain that'd only moments before been so bracing now seemed nightmarish. Why the fuck was I doing this to myself? I felt the clouds of despair creeping up, as if in answer to the turmoil in the sky above. This had been a stupid idea! I wasn't ready, physically or mentally.

Then, there it was. Off to one side of the path I was on, behind some foliage, what looked like concrete and brick. I took a closer look... yes! It was the entrance! I recognised it from the videos I'd watched! So much for trying to keep me from finding it, I thought.

I had a choice, I could go in now, see what I could find, or come back. On one hand I was desperate to get exploring and was about to step through the entrance when my leg jabbed with pain. Thank god it did, I realised I was knackered, unfit, in no way ready to go into a dark labyrinth.

I walked back to the path, gathering my thoughts. Yes, I had found the bunker, but no, I was in no state to go any further today. As my initial excitement ebbed away I recognised I would need help and equipment. At the very least I needed a torch, which I didn't have.

I went back to the four by four, turned on the engine, and let the hot air blower dry me out. Soon the outside world was obscured by the mist forming on the windows. I sat in my metal and plastic cocoon, pondering my next move. I would probably need some rope, definitely a camera, some waterproof clothing… I made a mental checklist as I flicked the heater from blowing on my feet to clearing the windscreen. By the time I pulled away, with a clear view of the way ahead, I knew what to do.

Knowing what I needed made planning for a return quick and easy. I spoke to members of my family, to friends, even to one of the people I'd tried to get hold of online. The latter was familiar with not only this site, but several others. I agreed a price for him to act as a guide across the locations he knew. A provisional date was set to return.

I couldn't believe my luck! Everything was falling into place. Or was it? Hindsight is a wonderful thing, and can make anything seem meaningful. Later I wondered if this had been fated, if this was always going to have happened.

5

The Descent into Fan Bay and a New Perception of Reality

It was mid-2009, the first trip planned. What would I find in those dark places? Would my entrance into them reflect my simultaneous psychological emergence into the light?

Nothing could have prepared me for what I encountered, not the events around my father's death, or Robin's return, nothing. Each step into the darkness took me further from the reality I'd so comfortably leaned on for my whole life. As the darkness rose up to meet me I was changed. The David Chapman entering the Fan Bay shelter remained forever in that darkness. The incarnation that emerged was a changed man.

The morning of the descent, my friend Alasdair, his son Matt, and I met our guide in Dover. A young man named Ian, he had proved his worth already by showing me around some other sites, including the Z Rocket. I had some general expectations based on my experiences in the other locations. There would be echoing concrete, the sound of water dripping, alongside an ever present sound of the wind. Alongside those noises I knew we would be able to hear something of the outside world.

I was wrong. It was silent inside! Completely, pin-drop, silent. And huge! I couldn't quite take in how massive it was. The scale overwhelmed me and I wandered along through the dark trying to take it all in.

As we rounded a bend in a tunnel my attention was snagged by writing on a stretch of exposed chalkface: 'Nobby Clark Royal Engineers 1942'. I stopped to look at this message from the past. Nobby Clark had stood here, all those decades ago and scraped his name into the soft rock. Who was he? Had he been working here because he was unable to go to the front? Maybe he'd seen action building fortifications elsewhere and was brought back from Europe? Had he made a dangerous journey to help construct part of our last defence against Hitler?

I snapped out of the moment and realised the other three had gone on ahead, indeed were now quite some way from me. I'd have to get a shake on to catch up with them. I opened my mouth to call after them, to ask them to hold up for me. Nothing came out.

Nothing.

A sudden and irrational terror gripped me. The temperature dropped and I felt frozen to the spot. I felt panic rise like the head on a poorly poured pint, frothing up uncontrollably, threatening to overtop my defences.

Then I heard a sound, heavy footsteps, crunching on the flakes of chalk that dusted the floor. The steps were slow, deliberate, only inches away. I felt as if I were being inspected, looked over by someone judging me.

I could feel a presence. Someone was there! Could another explorer have found me? I'd heard no-one coming in behind us, yet there was someone standing right next to me. I tried to speak again, finally forcing out "Come back, both of you, come back here!".

The presence snapped away, not a slow fading, no sense of departure, simply gone. Alasdair, Matt and Ian were with me moments later. Ian looked at me, shining his torch in my face, "What did you hear?". This perplexed me, did he know I might hear something in this monumental darkness? If so, why hadn't he said anything?

Watching the hours of video footage later I realised he had said something. We'd been so distracted by the wonder of the place we'd paid no attention to Ian telling us he thought the place was haunted. He'd not been overt in his warning, but watching the video it was clear he believed something dwelt in the darkness. His words made it clear he considered himself a ghost hunter! Why hadn't I picked up on this sooner? He had hunted, I'd become the haunted.

I lied to them in that dark tunnel, I told them nothing of the footsteps, nothing of the closeness I'd felt. Instead I invented a cracking sound from the ceiling, made up an unlikely story of being fearful of its collapse. I wanted to get out of there, and was profoundly relieved when they bought my fib.

As we made our way back up the many stairwells to the surface, I stopped to snap a few photographs. I stood in the upper first landing, my hands shaking, my heart racing, shock at what had happened coursing through my veins. How I calmed myself long enough to use the camera I don't know, but I'm glad I did.

Why? Because later, reviewing the pictures and video it was obvious that while our naked eyes had seen nothing, our cameras had picked up clear evidence of the supernatural. It was one of the stills from the upper landing. I opened it on the screen of my PC, and a cold prickling ran down my spine. There were faces! Three faces! Three leering gargoyle-like faces, one smiling! In another there was a bizarre looking tornado of light, tipped on its side.

I wanted to remain rational, to keep calm and not let my imagination run away with me. I tamped down my initial shock and called Alasdair. Perhaps he'd look at the photos and tell me the images were nothing more than artefacts of the camera reacting with the low-light in the tunnel?

I called his number, it was engaged. I waited for ten minutes, then tried again. No, still engaged. I had to speak to him! My patience had ebbed to nothing. As I slammed the phone down for the third time I realised I had no option but to drive over. I grabbed the camera, my keys, and headed for the door.

I was about to open it when there was a knock on the door. I opened it to an ashen faced Alasdair. He had his video camera gripped in his hands. He looked terrible, mumbled something about the footage, and pushed past me.

I calmed him with a cup of tea and he told me what had happened. Matt had been looking through footage from our earlier trip to the Z Rocket Deep Shelter and had captured something very strange. He plugged the camera into my PC and we scrolled through the footage. It showed two boys walking down the stairwell when a sudden flash of orange light appeared directly in front of them. It was no more than a handful of frames, the kind of thing that could be written off as lens flare. I looked at Alasdair quizzically, what was I supposed to see?

He played the footage in slow motion, dropping it right down to single frames as we neared the moment he wanted me to see.

I almost fell off my chair! There was an old man, smoking a pipe! I couldn't let him think it had only happened to him. I told him what I'd seen, sparing no details. What had we found? These were two different locations but very similar effects! I'd opened a can of worms, now I faced having to swallow them down.

We returned to the shelters, spending the next few days conducting tests. We hoped to capture something on film, Alasdair's idea. He's a professional photographer so had a lot of suggestions to reduce the likelihood of false positives. We let the cameras cool to the ambient temperature. I wondered why, maybe he wanted to rule out the risk of any condensation on the lenses? I didn't ask him, just followed his instructions.

The footage was disappointing, nothing but a brief moment of static on one of the video cameras. It was at the same spot as the boys had recorded the image of the old man but it wasn't enough to prove anything. We were hooked though, so went online and ordered some more specialist recording equipment. I contacted Ian to fill him in. He was oddly calm about the news and told me he could take me to some other places where we might be able to capture more interesting results. I readily agreed, not knowing what I would find.

We wanted to know, to learn more. We had passed the point of 'Do we really want to know about this stuff?', had made the step through the one-way door into needing to know. There are cliches about genies, bottles, crossing lines - all these would be easy to fall into, and all would be right. My view of the world was already changed, how much more could reality warp?

Could I put my previous ignorance down to inflexibility in thinking? Had all these things been happening around me for my whole life, lost to my eyes as my mind remained closed? Or has the knowledge that we're not ever truly alone been kept from us? Are there those who know but who choose to keep it from becoming public knowledge?

No doubt the sceptical reader will be laughing at me, ready with an explanation for everything I saw. The images on the video? Lens flare. The presence in the tunnel? A stiff breeze combined with the sounds of my companions carrying in the silent space. The smell of Robin? Nothing but an imagination run amok on a cocktail of pain and medication. There are explanations for everything, but not a single one is adequate.

I would have laughed at myself as well, I was a sceptic too! I would have laughed long and hard. But after everything I saw, the last laugh would have been on me. It's easy to mock these things when removed from them, but never underestimate the effects they have on your life or mind.

The events I've experienced have been terrifying, but that fear proves to me that I'm a normal person. I have chosen a path knowing many will struggle to walk it with me. Indeed many will struggle to believe anything I say as being true! I know this, yet I still walk that path.

I have no answers, I can't pretend to be able to tell you what everything I've experienced means. Is there life after death? Are there souls trapped in the liminal in-between spaces? Perhaps time will provide answers, perhaps it will not. All I can do is tell you what happened to me, tell you what I think these things mean and leave you to make your own mind up.

6

Eastry Hospital Hauntings

Ian recommended another site, a workhouse in east Kent, formerly owned by the Eastry Union Workhouse Infirmary. Over 122 years it had been put to many uses, ending in the mid-Nineties after some years as a mental hospital under the auspices of the NHS.

Ian was obviously rather strange. As we got to know him, it became more and more evident his obsession with the paranormal was almost unnatural. He seemed especially drawn to dangerously unstable abandoned locations. He claimed his dead father as the seat of his inspiration. A man who had taken his child to visit these sites, Ian's father had killed himself. Not just that, he'd done it at one of the sites Ian intended to take us to. He was intriguing though, his darker musings offset by his enthusiasm for historic sites, ghosts, and the TV show 'Most Haunted'. He was mono-maniacal in his obsession, nothing outside the arena of the supernatural interested him.

I wondered if this strange young man was merely emulating his television heroes. Maybe he fancied himself as a young Derek Acora, his obsession running no further than earnest copying. By the time we'd finished the investigation at the Workhouse, any illusions I'd clung to about him were resolutely shattered. Any doubts over what pulled his strings washed away in the light of what I experienced.

The evening of the visit began as a fleet of cars converged on the site. A large group of us, armed with freshly ordered equipment were set to find everything we could. We had digital dictaphones, condenser mics, cameras, video recorders and gauss meters, along with an array of wonderful gadgets. Any respectful paranormal investigator would be happy so tooled up for an evening lurking around dangerously derelict buildings! If only we'd packed our brain cells along with the waterproof bags, extra batteries, and wind mufflers.

Personally, I was increasingly driven by a need to solve the riddle of all that had happened since the departure of my Father. Specifically the events at Fan Bay and Z Rocket played on my mind, demanding my attention, demanding answers. Alasdair had struggled with what he'd seen, scepticism battling hard fact leaving him uncomfortably conflicted. I was not suffering at all, my days of supernatural scepticism were gone, burned away in the bright light of what I'd experienced over the last couple of years.

Armed with an amount of equipment that would have made the Ghostbusters blush, we'd collected our late night guide from his home in Dover. We convoyed to the Eastry site where we formed into small groups of two or three. We were ready to explore the sprawling site, to cover as much ground as possible. Each team had its share of equipment, voice recorders, video and stills cameras. Alasdair took it next level, he was armed with equipment to monitor electromagnetic fields and temperature fluctuations. I couldn't help feeling confident about our chances of success.

My confidence was well placed.

I wandered on my own, checking in with the teams roaming across the different floors and different wards. I'd made my way along a central corridor and then down the main stairs. I was heading for the video camera in the boiler room when Ian came barrelling out of a side door, his camera attached to a tripod held tight in his hands.

"Dave! Quick, come with me!"

I stood, looking at him, momentarily shocked into silence.

He looked at me, "What the fuck are you waiting for?"

"Er.. ok" I said, following him.

We went into a small side room, containing a few old bed frames. He locked off his video camera, aiming it into one of the corners.

"Ian?" I asked

"Hmmmhmmm?", he replied, distracted.

"Why am I here?"

"Oh, yeah, it's cos I'm scared of this room"

"Why??"

He didn't say anything but stared at me. The moment hung, becoming uncomfortable. At the point where I felt I could bear it no more, Alasdair called me to come upstairs.

As quick as my leg would let me I legged it up the stair, relieved to be away from the weird as all buggery vibe in the room with Ian. An excited Alasdair was waiting in one of the larger former wards. He grinned widely, handing me some equipment and asking me to scan the room temperature. I did as I was asked, swinging the probe around the room. As I neared one of those old-style free-standing modesty blinds (you know the ones, on wheels, designed to create a bit of privacy in a larger space) the temperature dropped. The background in the rest of the room had been a steady 18 degrees, but as I approached the blind it plummeted down to minus two! I couldn't believe what I was seeing, so scanned it again. Minus two again! Then, just as unexpectedly, the temperature shot straight back up to 18! Another member of the team, further away in the ward suddenly shouted, "It's over here now!" It was hard to believe what was happening, but the readings from the equipment were clear, something was moving around the room! It was as if it knew we were there and was trying to escape.

I was called for again, this time someone on the top floor yelled down. Leaving the team in the ward to take lots of video and photographs, and telling them I'd be right back, I, once more, hauled myself up the stairs. As I reached the top I heard Alison, my wife, and my sister, Jane calling for me. I could see them both in the diffuse cone of light my flashlight cast down the corridor, they both looked rattled.

"There's something here, Dave!" said Jane, Alison nodding in agreement. Jane pointed at a section of the room near a boarded-up window, "It's really really cold in this spot!"

I scanned the space, just as I had done on the floor below. the result was the same: background temperature sitting at 18 degrees with a dizzying plunge to less than zero in the corner. Could it be damp in the wall? I scanned around a little more, eighteen degrees everywhere else. I scanned the cold corner again… and it was now also eighteen degrees! There was no way I could argue with my sister or my wife, they were right: something was going on here!

"Turn on all the recording stuff" I said, "let's see if we can prompt a reaction!" With the dictaphone running and Alison snapping photo after photo, Jane deployed her great skill of pissing things off. Some might suggest that's something you should never do!

Jane stalked around the room, attempting to taunt whatever was there into reacting. "Come on! Show yourself! We know you're there! Alison here wants to take your photo! Dave wants to see you!" On and on she went, taunting, cajoling, almost insulting what was there. For a moment I felt lightheaded, then Jane cried out, "Oh my God, I'm freezing! I can feel ice going right up my legs!" she looked stricken, "Jesus, what am I standing on? Is it carpet, Dave, cos it feels soft and spongy!" The floor was solid wood from wall to wall, not even a rotting board to explain what she felt. What she described sounded as if space and reality were coming apart. It was like the bonds holding it all together were evaporating. Could the field that held it all in place be being manipulated beneath her feet?

Good God, had my sister become the first-ever interdimensional traveller without even realising!? Could something be manipulating the Higgs field, messing about with the Bosons binding matter into mass?

I later asked my friend Lionel Fanthorpe what his opinion was, he replied -

Dear Dave,

Further to our recent phone conversation, we have now had another very careful look at the material on the memory stick.

Firstly, there does definitely seem to be something abnormal here: the kind of anomalous phenomena that we love to study in A.S.S.A.P. Secondly, weird as it all is, we would emphasise that there is absolutely nothing to fear. The powers of light are infinitely stronger than the powers of darkness. We have nothing to fear but fear itself.

What might the images and sounds mean? What might be causing them?

The first possibility is that they are traces of departed human beings. If so, the worst they can do is to try to frighten us. They have absolutely no power at all to harm us.

Another possibility is that they are non-human psychic entities of some kind. Even if the manifestations are caused by what are popularly called demons or imps, again they have no power to do anything except to try to frighten us.

The third possibility is that manifestations of these types are from another dimension, or, perhaps, the result of time glitches. If time is susceptible to faults and breakdowns (the theological equivalent of earthquakes, but in time not in 3D matter) we might be able to see and hear something from the past while the breakdown lasts. They are only transitory things, and time seems to repair itself quite quickly. No ill effects from being there when it happens.

Once again, having studied the very interesting evidence again, we can positively assure you that there is absolutely nothing to fear.

Warmest wishes, prayers and blessings,
 As always,
 Your friend,
 Lionel

The night's investigation ended and the group returned to our cars. Jane, Alison, Alasdair, Matt and Ian all piled into my Discovery. We drove to Dover to drop Ian off at his mother's home. But something was off, something felt strange, everybody but Ian felt it.

Once in the town, we dropped Ian off, all congratulating one another on a successful evening. As soon as he was out of earshot the topic changed.

"What the fuck was that smell?" grimaced Jane, her face a mask of disgust.

Alison looked relieved, "Oh thank God! I thought I was imagining it!"

"You definitely weren't!" chipped in Matt.

I too had wondered if I was imagining it. The car'd been suffused with a stench of putridity all the way back. The sweet, cloying, musty stink of rot hadn't been there earlier. Had we brought something along with us? The conversation became hushed as we considered what might have hitched a lift. And what had become of it? The smell had gone when Ian got out of the car... had the spiritual attachment he'd picked up gone with him?

The next morning, after crashing out exhausted in the early hours, I began to look through the footage. I worked through it in the order we'd shot it and day was running into evening by the time I made it to the recordings of the top room. I heard Jane, demanding whatever was there show itself, her goading sounding even more needling on the video.

Then I heard it, something so shocking I tore my headphones off in disbelief. What the fuck!? I put the headphones back on and scrolled back along the timeline. I listened to it again: first, there was Jane saying "Come on! Show yourself! We know you're there! Alison here wants to take your photo! Dave wants to see you!", her voice rendered tinny by the headphones, then her further taunts and catcalls. A moment before she made her startled comment about being cold came the sound that had so shaken me. Clear as a bell, perfectly captured on the recording, a male voice said: "Fuck off!"

It wasn't anyone who was there! The voice slurred, either drunk or drugged, conveying a deep seated sorrow. I swear, I heard what I heard! I was stunned! I played it over and over, hearing it over and over. That voice, that awful voice, using its moment to tell my sister to "Fuck off!" Surely my ears were deceiving me? No! It was a human voice. Then I remembered, when Jane had goaded the spirit into revealing itself, the words 'Fuck off!' had formed in my mind. The voice on the recording came a moment after I had thought it.

I suppose the only moral I could take from this was that you should never mess with things you don't understand. I had been a sceptic, now I was faced with the undeniable facts that a reality beyond my comprehension, beyond my control, had more power than I'd ever thought possible.

I thought of the Bible, a book I hold no store in, a book designed by men to enslave man. Despite my attitude I knew I shouldn't disregard it entirely, even a poorly presented map can guide you to safety! I considered Ephesians chapter 6, verse 12

> *"For we wrestle not against flesh and blood, but against principalities, against powers, against the rulers of the darkness of this world, against spiritual wickedness in high places"*

Could the being in the ward have projected its words into the minds of living flesh and blood? What damage could that do? What damage could it have done to me?? Was there a spirit picking off neurons one at a time? What had I uncovered!

I must have played the recording more than a hundred times before calling Alasdair. I told him to go though all his recordings carefully, to listen to everything with an open ear and mind. A few hours later he was at my door, looking as shocked as he'd done before. He came in and played me selections of his own recordings. They were of the room Ian had seemed so terrified of, I rapidly realised why Alasdair was so shaken.

The recording clearly held four voices! But there had only been Ian and Alasdair in the room! I felt sick with fear: these weren't random words like most EVPs. The voices were responding to what Ian and Alasdair said. The two of them heard nothing in the room, but the copper coils of the microphones had caught it all. On the recording I heard Alasdair asking Ian why he was locking off the camera. His reply was overlaid with a second voice! While Ian said "To try to catch something" a voice on top said "What does *he* want me to say?" to which a second, less human, voice replied "I can kill you"

We continued to listen, finding so much more. One of them, in reaction to Jane's taunting, said, clear as day, "Can you stop her, please?". This plea to shut my sister up was entirely reasonable, I too had wanted her to stop!

The recording that freaked me out properly though was the last, a voice saying "Jesus's birth". What did it mean? I've pondered that incomplete recording for years: what about the birth of Jesus? What was the spirit trying to tell us? I can't even go back and check the audio, the hard drive it was on failed soon afterwards and now sits in a drawer. It is likely I will never know.

Alasdair refused to accept the reality of the situation, throwing himself into attempts at debunking. But I knew, I was certain, I'd see and heard too much. My world view shredded, I was forced to accept the truth. Alasdair looked for logical explanations and wanted to go back to retrace our steps to see if he could find them. I agreed, so we returned to the sites, allowed the cameras to reach room temperature, and recorded again.

Nothing. There was no evidence of anything that could have caused the phenomenon we'd experienced.

He tried tests to debunk the audio recordings but again failed. He realised he couldn't explain everything away and finally agreed with me. We had encountered the paranormal!

We contacted all kinds of self-styled paranormal investigators, finding most to be morons, con artists, or woo merchants. Not one of them understood what we were on about, and we found their reactions frustrating in the extreme. One group even accused us of faking the evidence! It was clearly a hoax, they insisted, the recordings being too clear. We realised we were alone

Halloween fast approached. I hatched a plan to make or break any doubts about what we'd seen. I'll regret that decision for the rest of my life.

7

Samhain 2009

The Detached Bastion in Dover was an abandoned Napoleonic era fort and Ian had never stopped banging on about it. He was obsessed, speaking of rumours of satanic rituals and devil worship happening there. The ritual locations even had names; "Old Smokey", "Devil's Alley", or even "Dead Man's Island". Despite the names sounding like so much made up bullshit, I was desperate to know more. I knew I should stay away, especially after what had happened before, but I was driven to uncover what truth I could find.

In a lot of ways, I could understand Ian's obsessions, even as I semi-mocked him. I was mesmerised by what we'd experienced so far on this dark path and had to know more. Was this how Ian's monomania had begun? If it was, I completely understood him. In this state of mind, I decided Halloween was the perfect night to visit the Z Rocket Deep Shelter then the Bastion.

The Detached bastion, Halloween 2009: rushing in where even

angels fear to tread!

The Z Rocket Deep Shelter is in St Margaret's Bay, near the Port of Dover. We were already familiar with it, Alasdair's son had, along with mine, captured the manifestation of the old man here some weeks earlier. Our group made our way down the steep slope towards the entrance. We made our way along the approach tunnel cut high in the cliff, leading to the main complex. My nerves buzzed and my heart rate climbed as I descended into the darkness.

What awaited in the darkness? I felt dizzy with anticipation. There was a certainly something unearthly hiding in the dark. I thought of the dog walkers strolling up above, taking in the view of the Channel unaware of the complex below.

We reached the main complex and made our way towards the stairwell where the old man had been seen. Almost immediately strange things started happening. The gauss meters peaked off the scale and the fully charged video camera batteries discharged. A solitary camera remained in working order as we filmed the stairwell, capturing nothing but electrical static. As our equipment failed two of the group said they could smell tobacco.

Was this it? Were we going to capture some evidence? No, there was nothing more. I felt my fear drain away, replaced with an abiding sense of disappointment. I felt crushed, defeated, saw myself as a failure. I told the others this site was a bust and that we should leave. Perhaps the Detached Bastion would grant us better luck?

8

We Enter into The Belly of The Beast

The moat at the Detached Bastion was a dark, dismal place at ten at night. It was overgrown and empty water bottles littered the place. There were hundreds of them! What the hell? Why were there so many?

We made our way through the darkness, along a small but well-worn path winding through the trees and bushes. It terminated at a small plate steel hatch, six or seven feet up a wall. We wrestled a log over and used it as a makeshift ladder. Alasdair scrambled up, disappearing into the darkness, then reappeared beckoning for us to hand up the equipment and bags. Once everything was through the hatch we each climbed up. The site felt even more spooky than it had last time we'd visited: the dark making the creeping ivy crawling all across the structure look like tentacles. It was as if the whole site had been smothered by a leviathan from the darkest depths.

Standing in the huge gallery on the other side of the hatch, my eye was drawn to the Satanic symbols painted on every surface. 'Demons!', 'Satan Lives', pentagrams, inverted crosses; all jostled for my attention. Holy shit, there were so many! They were on every surface, stretching off into the darkness.

Within minutes of entering the place the two women in the group complained of having difficulty breathing. Both felt as if there were a pressure or a weight in the centre of their chests. The remaining three of us felt nothing - the structure was well ventilated, riddled with open gun ports. I couldn't understand what they were talking about.

We set up the dictaphones and video recorders, new batteries inserted, then set off into the tunnels. We were on the path known as Devil's Alley, a long dark passage to the space nicknamed Dead Man's Island. The experience at the Z Rocket site had dented my hope and my expectations were low, as a result I felt relaxed, unphased by the place. Alasdair appeared similarly unconcerned and wandered off on his own to photograph the well in Devil's Cave.

I didn't even notice he'd dropped back from the group until six minutes later, when the top-of-his-lungs scream echoed down the tunnel. Jesus! What was going on? I whirled around, trying to pinpoint which direction the scream had come from and saw the flash of his torch bobbing up and down around 300 yards away. He was shouting "Dave! Dave!" his voice echoing in strange ways as he pelted down the passage.

As he shouted I could hear metal scraping on the ground, a distant sound grinding away beneath his yelling. He barrelled out of the tunnel, half out of his mind with fear. Never in my life had I seen him so terrified. As I tried to calm him, he kept repeating "I'm freaking out! I'm fucking freaking out!" He looked at me, his eyes wide with animalistic fear. Then he looked down, down to the camera on its tripod which had been bashing against the floor and walls as he'd run. He'd been so scared he'd not even concerned himself with protecting his £2000 camera.

His explanation for what had happened transformed my disappointment into fear.

"Alasdair! What the hell happened?"

"I was taking a slow exposure shot..."

"Of the well?"

"Yes, of the well", he shot me a look for interrupting, "So, I was taking the picture, feeling fine about being alone. I wanted to get some nice shots for my website..." he tailed off.

The rest of us stood in a loose circle around him, waiting for him to continue. The gap stretched to thirty seconds, then a minute, I lost my patience, "What happened??"

"I suddenly felt like I wasn't alone. I felt terror, and worse I felt I was being drained"

"Drained?" I echoed.

"Yeah, drained of life, like my life was being drained away. I couldn't move, I was so scared, I was sure someone was standing right in front of me, right up in my face! It was overwhelming, crushing, like oppressive, you know what I mean?"

I knew all too well what he meant, I'd felt the same during on that previous outing. A flash of cold ran down our collective spines, each of us flinging at the same instant. I looked from face to face, all showed fear. We were not alone here!

I was even more determined to press on now. We were onto something and I was not going to be frightened off. We composed ourselves, then continued down the eerie passageway deeper into the Bastion. The situation escalated almost immediately. Sounds echoed up from the distance, bouncing off the walls and doubling then tripling with each reflection. Soon a swirling miasma of shrieks and hoots surrounded us.

I glimpsed movement. My head whipped round, my eyes seeking out the tiniest clue of what I'd sensed. There! In the shadows, a dark figure running up the stairs down the corridor. I shouted out and ran after, reaching the foot of the stairs before I had time to think what I was doing.

I slowed as I climbed the stairs, which turned out to be a good thing. The stairs went nowhere! A wall filled the arch at the top, the path ahead long ago bricked up! The figure was gone as if it had never been there!

I turned, "He's gone! Did any of you video that?"

"I did!" replied Alasdair and turned the camera to face me. He pressed play... and the screen went black, a red battery icon flashing once in the instant before.

We went on, reaching the far end of another section of the vast complex. The tunnel ahead had caved in, forcing us to get down on hands and knees to pass through into the next series of rooms. What were we thinking? As when I'd run after the figure minutes before I didn't stop to consider how dangerous this route was! We each crawled through, ignoring the risk of further collapse in the tunnel above. It was a kind of insanity, I guess, a mania driving us forward, perhaps even something else pulling us.

On the other side, the rooms took a far more sinister turn. A hook swung on the end of a length of new looking blue nylon rope, hanging from the shadows high above us. What was it for? I could easily imagine someone tied up, their bound wrists held on that hook. I shivered.

The walls were covered in Satanic symbols, inverted crosses and triangles with a 6 scrawled at each point. Elsewhere, in red paint, someone had daubed 'Earth', 'Air', 'Fire' and 'Water', while 'Evoke the Spirit' was clear to see on another surface. Pentagrams, along with the words 'WitchCraft' and 'Satan' completed the effect.

Fuck! This place was seriously creepy! We couldn't stand to stay more than ten, maybe fifteen minutes. We returned through the collapsed section of the tunnel, again ignoring the potential danger. I was the first to go through.

As I did I stepped on something. There were a dozen or so water bottles on the floor! They'd not been there a quarter of an hour earlier, there was no way we could have missed them! Once we were all through, my son looked at the bottles littering the floor, "Should I pick these up, Dad?"
 "No, I think you should leave them" I replied.
 "Are you sure? They're all opened!"
 I felt there was something very wrong, so repeated myself.

Pausing only to again replace the batteries in the video cameras, we went back along Devil's Alley. As we walked we kept the dictaphones running, capturing the audio and snapped photos along the way. Once more we heard sounds ahead of us, this time I swung my powerful Lenser torch up quickly enough to make out a small group of people in cloaks running away!

I was beyond spooked! Who were these people? I could only assume we'd disturbed their Samhain plans. I have no idea how we remained calm, looking back I am astonished I didn't leg it right then and there. Instead of running, we made our way outside to the top of the fort. There, two small buildings squatted in the dark, old gun emplacements, around midnight we entered one and drank some coffee. Like I say, we were unnaturally calm given what we'd just seen!

The fresh night air further chased away any feelings of fear. How could there possibly be anything here to harm us! What a ridiculous idea, I scoffed! We were in Kent, for Christ's sake, not some catacombs under Paris! We decided we'd go back down into the Bastion, back down through a corroded and weather-worn hatch after passing across a small drawbridge.

At the moment we reached the hatch, my sister said, out of nowhere, "I wonder if anything is behind us?" She raised her voice, jokingly, "Are you following us?" She thought it was hilariously funny, but those words would haunt me later.

She took photos of us as we came through the archway back into the main structure and Alison continued to film with one of the video cameras. We trudged back to the way we'd come in, crossed back over the moat, and back to the cars.

So much for Hallowe'en! Sure, Alasdair had been spooked and we'd seen those hooded figures. But had we seen anything truly spooky? Not really, plastic bottles of water don't exactly count as a sighting of a ghost! The figures and the noises we'd heard had been nothing more than kids messing about. This was how I was able to rationalise everything that had happened, even the dying camera batteries didn't seem like a big deal as we drove away.

We had no idea what was going to happen to us. I had no way of knowing the 31st of October, 2009 was to be the last night of restful sleep I would ever experience.

9

The Revelation

The next morning, as I sat downstairs drinking my morning coffee, the phone rang. It was Jane, my sister, "Dave, I've been looking through the photos from last night, you've got to see these!"

I sipped my coffee, looked out the window at the crisp November morning, "What's up? What've you found?" I asked.

"It's the pictures I took after I was joking about someone following us, when we were coming through that arch, look I can't really explain. I'll email you the pictures right away."

I moved over to my desk, started the PC and sat with growing impatience as the machine slowly sparked to life. After what seemed like an eternity, I logged into my email and downloaded the pictures. There were three of them, all three appearing utterly nondescript on first inspection. Why had she wasted my time with these duds, I wondered. Then I noticed some bloody weird stuff in the background.

In one of the photos a bald, bulbous headed thing was blowing a kiss at the camera. I hadn't expected this, the first picture had been nothing more than bricks, stone, us, but this, this was something else entirely. The third picture was even more astounding.

Jane had fumbled the 'Party Flash' mode on when she'd taken the photos causing the camera to take a rapid burst of three shots. These were what she'd sent. I sat back, this meant the second and third photos were taken only fractions of an instant after the first! Where the hell had the bulbous headed thing appeared from? For, make no mistake, it had simply appeared. There was no sign of it in what I now recognised as the first frame, then it was there in the second! In the third things got even weirder!

I called Alasdair. He drove over as soon as he could. I wanted his opinion on what I was looking at: he was a good photographer and would be able to tell me if my mind was playing tricks, seeing monsters in lens flare or dust. He agreed there was more to these photos than we'd initially thought. In fact it looked like we'd surprised the being by using the 'Party Flash'! Had it thought it was safe once the first flash had popped? Maybe it was cheekily blowing a kiss at the camera to mock that we'd missed him? But we hadn't! My sister's hamfistedness had caught him out, and now here he was, captured in the final two images!

More was to be uncovered in these photos, weeks later when we were contacted by a radio station called Haunted Cornwall FM, but for now I was overwhelmed with what had happened. I'd been so calm the night before! I'd laughed off the cloaked figures and the howling noises as kids messing about, I'd never considered that the real malice might be hiding in the dark, unseen by all but the camera. Fuck me! Jane had tricked a demon! At least that's what I later decided, after years of mulling over what happened. This was no joke, I wish it were. I wish the things that happened afterwards had been the punchline to a gag told by Jane.

10

The Night Visitor

At one minute to midnight, as the final moments of November 1st 2009 ticked away, I woke. What pulled me from my sleep was a familiar nightmare, one that had traumatised me for five or six years, but which hadn't returned since I was nine. As a child I would always wake from it in a state of unbridled terror, panic gripping my boyhood mind.

I had tried to explain the nightmare to my mother, but my infant tongue hadn't the words necessary to convey the darkness of my nighttime horrors. I was an innocent child, lacking everything I needed to adequately explain what was happening to me in my sleep. Now I was an adult, this time I fully understood the entire context of this long ago forgotten childhood late night tormentor. This beast from my past returned to me.

I have no right to expect you to buy into this, to accept my word. All I can tell you is these things happened to me.

I lay in the darkness, wide awake, the terrifying flashback rapidly fading despite the bass drum thrum of my heart, beating so fast I could well imagine it bursting from my chest. My hair was drenched with sweat, plastered to my head, a wet clinging mess. I blinked a couple of times, waiting for my eyes to adjust. Why was it so dark? It wasn't just dark, it was a smothering pitch blackness. No light anywhere, as if the thickest blackout curtains hung across the windows.

I realised with a shock I wasn't alone. I was dimly aware of Alison sleeping next to me, but the presence I felt wasn't her. It was right up in my face, watching me. I felt drained of energy and then realised why this seemed so familiar… it was what Alasdair had gone through the previous night! In fact, it was what I'd encountered in the Fan Bay Deep Shelter!

As I thought more about it I recognised the obvious - these things, these beings, like to wait until they sense vulnerability. And vulnerable I was! I was paralysed! It wasn't sleep paralysis though, I was wide awake. No, it was terror. The dread built, crushing and smothering me, I felt like I would die. Then, a break in the suffocation, a second of release. I dived for the bedside light, grabbing wildly at it, fumbling for the switch. It came on!

Light filled the room, but then died immediately. The bulb buzzed, then strobed, flashing the room. Alison woke, "Dave? What's going on? What's happening? Why's the light doing that?" I was now fully able to move so jumped up to the main light switch. That too began to flicker and flash. Did we have a problem with the electrics?

I went onto the landing, flicking the wall switch on as I passed it... the light began to strobe! I looked back into the bedroom and stopped short: all was normal! The lights, the overhead, the bedside lamp, both shone steadily. If this was a wiring problem it was following me around the house.

And then, just like doesn't happen in films, I needed a piss. I couldn't believe it! Of all the times for my bladder to speak up for itself! The landing light was still flickering, but the bathroom light came on and stayed on. As I relieved myself I pondered on this: why wasn't this bulb flickering? Washing my hands it hit me, it was a flourescent tube. The other bulbs were standard, basic things, but the bathroom light was different.

My fear was starting to evaporate, the novelty of what was going on with the lights fascinating me. My terror was turning into intrigue. I went down to the kitchen, made two cups of coffee and went back to Alison. For the next hour the two of us sat up in bed and watched the creep-show buzz and flash around us. Then, as abruptly as it had started it stopped.

It is a miracle we fell asleep, yet we did. Already I was feeling that no-one and nothing would run me out of my home.

That following morning I phoned Alasdair. He was enthralled as I told him of the previous night's bizarre goings-on. Once he had pumped me for every last detail he asked if I'd had chance to look at the footage from the Detached Bastion. I had to confess I hadn't, I'd been somewhat overwhelmed I told him.

He had listened to some of the dictaphone recordings, and wanted me to listen.

What I heard was very odd and deeply troubling. When the full recording was reviewed we found EVPs. Listening gave me a feeling of sickness, like you feel in the moment you realise you've done something that's going to be awful but can do nothing to stop it.

I will try to explain as best I can. It was as we came out of Devil's Cave and found the bottles of water. As my son asked whether he should pick them up we'd captured a low frequency EVP. Initially we couldn't work out what we were listening to but after Alasdair ran the audio through some software we heard clearly. The full gravity of what I was not only hearing but understanding shook my world. It was the same as we'd captured in the abandoned hospital. But instead of telling us to "fuck off" this voice did something far weirder. A moment before I told my son to leave the water where it was the ultra-low frequency EVPs said the same words! It was as if I were echoing them!

What could this mean? There was no mistaking what we'd recorded: the EVPs were speaking my words before I said them. It made me wonder, are human affairs orchestrated by some unseen non-human force? Or can the human mind project thoughts onto modern recording devices? Sceptics can take the much favoured overplayed easy route, declare us hoaxers or even insane but who gives a damn about them? I have found these types of people have the most to lose, the most to hide. They don't want any of this to be true. An afterlife, ghosts, demons... all point to the most feared thing any human being could imagine: a "Creator". Not only that, but accountability for our deeds both good and bad. Think about that for a moment. A judge where no dodgy lawyers could be of any use, where every deed is laid bare for all to see and know.

A few months later, I told my brother Michael of the conclusion I'd reached after hearing the EVPs. In turn he told me of an old couple who had lived in his street. Happily married for sixty years, the wife was astonished, one day while gardening, to be hit over the head with a lump hammer. Surviving the assault she was even more surprised to discover her attacker was her husband. He'd gone into his shed, picked up the hammer, then whacked her. When the police arrived he claimed he had no recollection of any of it.

Had a force controlled him? Was it like the night in the Detached Bastion where the evil force had spoken my words a moment before I did? I know first hand what happens when something external directs words and deeds.

Earth, wind, fire, water.

All is linked, all is made of the same stuff. You memories, personality, thoughts, feelings, emotions, desires: all are energy. Electrical signals passing between neurons in your brain. Those signals can be altered, basic drugs, even electromagnetic fields can change our perception. Is it so ridiculous to imagine unseen realms could influence us?

Look back through human history. In every culture you will find accounts of this kind of phenomenon. Were they all crazy? How many times have you sworn an oath or gone to a church wedding or funeral? Why do you celebrate Christmas or Easter, derived from Pagan festivals? People are in such willful ignorance!

I didn't believe: I was the same as you. But once I had seen what I would before consider impossible, I had to look for answers. We humans are such arrogant creatures but the truth is we know nothing of the world around us.

11

3rd November 2009, 3 am on the Dot!

We had pissed something off when we'd gatecrashed Halloween 2009. Our uninvited, unwelcome interruption had angered whoever was holding the late night ritual. That Samhain we'd inadvertently disturbed the actions of others. I later discovered people were often seen coming and going from the site, late at night. Groups of people, cloaked and mysterious had been seen by locals over the decades. The descriptions I heard in the following months and years matched exactly what my group had seen, weird cloaked figures far in the distance. Perhaps it was they who'd brought in the bottles of water?

Was the water intended for a more nefarious purpose? Christianity has Holy Water but so does the inversion of Witchcraft and Devil worship! I say 'inversion', for Devil Worship is a direct inverting of the mythos of Christianity. They use an inverted cross as an icon, have a love of church buildings, and have their own twisted spiritual water. Where the hours between 1 pm and 3 pm hold a special place in the story of the Crucifixion, so the hours of 1 am to 3 am do for the Devil worshipper.

Is this even true? Is what I've recounted above nothing but bullshit, passed through chinese whispers? Who knows? All I can do is tell you what I know. The right or wrong of the information is for you to debate over.

At 3 am, on the 3rd of November 2009 I woke again from my childhood terror. Once more I was drenched in sweat, my heart hammering in my chest. The room was awash with a shifting silver light, diffuse and yet sharp at the same time. It took me a moment to realise it was the television. The screen showed the static howl caused by the echo of the Big Bang. Only now does it strike me how odd this was; our TV, like any other modern box, shows a blue screen when there's no recognised signal! I should not have been looking at the shifting snowstorm dancing across the screen.

Alison woke, a perplexed, sleepy, look on her face. "Why are you watching a blank TV screen, Dave?"

The words "I'm not" had barely passed my lips when the room plunged into sudden darkness, the TV switching abruptly off. I sat, stunned, the afterimage of the screen floating in front of my eyes in the dark. Had we been lying on the remote? Had Alison accidentally turned the TV off when she'd propped herself up to get a better look at what was happening? No, the remote was where it always was, on the bedside cabinet.

Then the lights erupted into their strobe light show. This was now the third night in a row, and I was no longer in any mood to deal with this supernatural nonsense. "Oh, for Christ's sake, just piss off!" I shouted, before leaping up and unplugging the TV and all the lights. Darkness once again reigned in our bedroom, the presence robbed of its tools for the night.

After the same thing happened the following night, I remembered the bathroom light being the only one unaffected. The next morning I went around the house, collected the old filament bulbs replacing them with fluorescents. The TV stayed unplugged when the lights went out. Problem solved?

No, problem transferred!

It spread to the others who'd been there on that night at the Bastion, and then out to some who were only tangentially linked! Alasdair, my wife, my son… all had things happen to them. Fair enough, perhaps, they'd been there at the Bastion. But my brother, Michael? My mother? No, neither of them had yet this malevolence attached itself to them as well.

Even my dog, a fierce German Shepherd called Oscar went crazy one night, howling more like a wild wolf than a domesticated pet. On other nights he ran up and down the stairs, as if playing with someone, his frantic dashing playmate seemingly only visible to him.

We were looking after my mother back then. She'd been with us since the death of my father, two and a half years earlier. She was the most honest, most kind, most downright decent soul I've ever known. Yeah, I know, we all say this of our mothers, but she truly was someone very special indeed. Kind to a fault, she would give away her last penny or morsel of food if she felt someone needed it more than her.

So it horrified me that she too became a victim of these odd encounters. It was mid November, the year drawing in and the house lit now solely by fluorescent bulbs. I was sat at the desk where my computer was when she cried out, "David! David!" She was pointing up into the corner of the room, directly above my head, "Can you see it??"

I swivelled around on my chair, "What is it, mum?"

"Above you!"

I looked back at the wall, at the ceiling, there was nothing there. "What's above me, mum?"

"It's like a cloud, a face..."

"What? A cloud, a face?" I turned to face her.

"Yes, David! A face, made of cloud! No, there are two faces!"

I looked away from her and back to the wall. I could still see nothing, but I felt the hair on the back of my neck pricking up. "What are they doing, mum?"

"They're looking right at you, they look angry"

On another occasion, she came running out of her bedroom. She had been thinking how she needed to eat more, and had heard a voice say "Yes, you should". The next day she came out of her bedroom around the same time, and told me she'd heard applause when she was making her bed. She had terrible arthritis in her hands and found everything hard to do, was a spirit mocking her?

Not long after this, she was watching TV when she turned and said "David, did you hear that?"

"Did I hear what, mum?"

"I thought I heard a man say something to me. He sounded like he was having a conversation with me."

"What did he say?"

"I don't know, David! It sounded like a foreign language to me!"

My imagination was fired, things were getting all too real. I began to fear what might happen next, and listened to my mum's suggestion. She had been a God-fearing woman all her life, and said we should ask for help from the church. A few years before, I would have laughed at the idea of bringing an exorcist into my life, but I now knew how real all this was.

12

A Desperate Plea for Help

We went to church. The only one I knew was the Roman Catholic church in Canterbury. As a school boy at the strict St. Thomas's Catholic School, I was forced to go, so it seemed to be the obvious choice.

As Alasdair and I drove up outside I thought to myself "Ok, let's do this thing right, let's get help from the holy knights of God'. Surely a sanctuary from evil such as a church would be safe? We parked, and grabbing the folder of photographs we'd brought along, made our way inside.

My eyes were still adjusting to the darkness when a black clad priestly looking figure approached us. "Can I help you, my son?"
 I looked at Alasdair then at this apparition of holiness, "I hope so, Father, I very much hope so"
 He nodded slightly, and smiled, "You can call me David"

He wasn't a Father, it turned out, rather a Deacon and he did his best to help. First I showed him the photographs. He shuffled through them, a look of concern passing across his face. He looked up, "Is this the face of evil? I need to show these to a colleague, please wait here." With that he rushed off to the back of the church, clearly attempting not to look like he was wanting to go faster than he was.

We stood around, waiting. I looked at my surroundings. Now my eyes had adjusted I could admire just how elegant yet simple the interior was. Great pale arches soared from their bases on squat pillars, the circular stained glass an inescapable focal point. It was a far cry from the dingy darkness of the Detached Bastion, that was for sure!.

Deacon David returned, "I've spoken to the Cannon, can you tell me all about what happened?" I gave him the bullet-point version, laying out the salient facts as I best recalled. He nodded throughout, occasionally interrupting to seek clarification on this or that point. At the end he looked me straight in the eye and asked "What do you think I could do to help?"

"I need you to come to my house, Dave" I said, "do whatever it is you people do to get this weird stuff out of my home."

"Well…" he replied, drawing the word out to give a clear impression of discomfort, "I can do that, but it's not like in the films, just so you know"

"That's fine, Father" I said, not caring that I'd used the wrong title, "All I need is my home back to normal."

He didn't show.

We waited and waited. He'd agreed to come, he'd given his

word he would come, so where the hell was he? He'd promised! He'd kept the photos, so I assumed he was going to give them back when he arrived at my house. Now I was out of pocket, the pictures had cost a mint to get blown up.

A few weeks later, out in town shopping, my wife and I saw a little fuzzy haired priest coming the other way. "Hello, Father David", I said, "what happened to you then?"

The man of God blanched, his first attempts to speak nothing but splutters and hesitant noises. When he managed to compose himself he squeaked out "Oh, Dave, yes, um... I'm sorry about that, I've been meaning to get in touch with you."

"Really?" I said, barely able to hide my scepticism at this claim.

"Yes... um... well, I'm sorry to say I think I might be out of my depth on this"

I sighed. "Okay Father David, is there anyone in your church who wouldn't be out of their depth?"

But the Deacon was already on the move, speeding up as he worked his short legs to put distance between us. He looked back over his shoulder, "I'm sorry, I'll be praying for you", and he was gone.

So much for the church! The church that had been so happy to receive money from my mother when she'd struggled to bring up four kids on next to nothing. She'd been there for them, were they now there for us? Were they fuck! I was furious. God forbid you ever find yourself in the same situation, but if you do you'll get more help from your local pizza place than from this shower! At least with a pizza you'll have a tasty snack to chomp down on while being terrorised by the forces of darkness!

As I pondered on this encounter with Deacon David I began to think I'd met him before. Then it came to me, it had been when my father had died. The undertaker had asked what our faith was and then suggested the ideal Catholic priest for the job. It was only fucking Deacon David! I'd even given him a speech to read out at the graveside, he'd said it was better than anything he could have written! This made me even more angry. Oh yes, the church were fine when it came to taking money, but when you need help? When you need them not to shaft you? Can't see them for dust.

My sister suggested we try Eastry Church. It was close to where she lived and near to the hospital where we'd had that early encounter. Her suggestion was perfect, and we met the woman who would go on to become a dear friend of the family, Reverend Diane Johnson.

Diane welcomed us all into her home and we set about telling her our creepy story. Then we showed her the photos. This lady was right on the ball from the word go! She was shaken by the photos, repeatedly exclaiming "Oh no!" as she looked at them closely. Why had Deacon David not spotted any of this? Do evil dishonest people only see what they want to see in these odd photos? Did I dare to imagine Deacon David was actively evil, knowingly dishonest? Is it possible only the truthful, the decent, the honest can see the truth?

Diane told us about her past. She had worked as an exorcist for the Anglican church, only retiring when the stress of the position became too much for her. She was no stranger to what she called "dark forces" and referred us to her successor, the Reverend Amanda Evans. Reverend Evans got back to us almost immediately - a far cry from the behaviour of Deacon David!

The first thing Reverend Evans told me to do took me by surprise: I was to destroy all trace of the EVPs and all the photos! She didn't even want to look at them, despite the excitement of her companion, an eager young man called Steven. It can't be said they didn't go the whole nine yards with the exorcism though! My family and I cringed from embarrassment when they turned up in broad daylight and started praying at the front door! They went from door, to driveway, to garden fence, Bible held proudly in front of them as they loudly read from it. Then they came into the house and prayed over my computer! I don't think Bill Gates would have considered that an appropriate debugging technique! I'm certain he wouldn't have approved of the Holy water they flicked hither and thither around the house. Jesus! This was so awful! What must the neighbours have thought?

It is strange that I thought this way, and maybe uniquely British. Here we were, getting nightly visits from what I was convinced was an evil spirit and I was more concerned about what my neighbours would think! Surely a little embarrassment was a small price to pay considering what was going on?

I'd love to be able to report how successful the exorcism was, how worthwhile the toe-curling embarrassment had been, but I can't. After watching this ritual cleaning of the house with baited breath we'd expected our lives to go back to normal. But no, if anything things were worse! Far from driving out evil, it seemed we'd pissed it off.

13

The Radio Show

I received an email from Haunted Cornwall FM asking if I'd be happy to appear on one of their shows. What would be the harm? I thought, so replied that I'd gladly appear.

During the show, live on air, one of the two hosts asked me to look at some of the photos I'd sent them. Ignoring the requests of the Anglican exorcist, I'd not deleted them and soon had them up on screen. "Look at the archway" the main host said, directing my attention to one of the burst of photos Jane had taken at the Bastion, "What do you see?"

Fuck.

How had I not noticed that before? There, clear as day, was an orb of light. I had never seen it before, and I'd looked at that photo dozens of times. "There's an orb" I said, voice trembling with the wonder of it all.

"Yeah, there is", he said, "but forget about that, look down"
"Fucking hell!"

"Dave!" the other host laughed, "remember we're live on air!"

"Oh yeah, sorry" I said, but my attention wasn't on what they were saying, my attention rested entirely with the dog in the photo. There was a dog, in the photo, looking straight at the camera!

The next two hours seemed to last forever, as the radio host showed me more and more things I'd not noticed in the photograph. I would have thought it were a trick if it weren't for the fact I was on my own computer, looking at my own files. Why hadn't I seen these things? Could it be I had been dishonest, an evil person myself, thus denied access? Was publicly admitting to what I'd seen enough for me to now be honest and truthful? Was that why my eyes were now opened?

The hosts talked of orbs, of elemental spirits, of all manner of things I didn't yet understand. I began to zone out, letting the meaningless words wash over me. Then I was snapped back suddenly. "We think you might be a developing Medium", said the main presenter.

I stifled a laugh. Oh boy, what the living fuck was I doing on this radio show with this pair of nutcases? I imagined myself backing away from a rabid animal, maintaining eye contact until I was safely able to run.

But then some of the things they said rang true. "Whatever you do, Dave, don't go to a Christian church for help, it'll only make it worse." No shit, Sherlock! They knew I'd spoken to both the Catholics and the Anglicans, and they knew nothing had been chased from my house.

Their gallop of information was, in all honesty, overwhelming. They said so much to me it's hard to remember it all now. They wanted me to try to get more EVPs and talked about remote writing. I can't pretend that this shit was all too freaky for me.

As I write now, many years later, I am much wiser, more clued up. I understand more about theology, the occult, even demonology. Now I can look back on this radio appearance and realise that what I laughed at was nothing funny.

The bizarre goings-on continued unabated. Michael, my brother, came around and mum told him about everything that had been happening. My brother was a cynic, the personification of a Doubting Thomas and wasted no time in expressing his caustic ridicule. We were idiots to believe this bullshit, he told us, He spared us no cruelty, going about the balloon of our beliefs with a sharpened pin of sarcasm and mockery.

Fate had a different idea for Michael, though. Mum was trying to explain to him what she'd seen and he was laughing at her, telling her she'd imagined it all. She stood her ground, adamant in her belief. Michael was becoming more and more amused, I could see he was about to start laughing. Suddenly, with a loud crash, the heavy brass clock that stood in the middle of the coffee table in the living room fell on its face.

We all stopped talking. The clock had three feet, was balanced firmly on the table, no one had touched it. Yet there it was, lying face down without anyone touching it. He couldn't deny this, he couldn't pretend to have not seen it! I looked at him, his face was pale, like he'd seen something of pure evil. He sat looking at the clock for a few minutes, then stood up, "Okay, yeah, I've got to go now". Then he was gone. He did not return for over a month.

Even now he refuses to believe what his eyes showed him, his comfort zone impenetrable.

14

Holiday Hauntings

In July 2018 my brother Michael and his new partner Katie took a two week holiday to Alicante. They stayed in my nephew's apartment, and very quickly things took a weird turn. On the second night they were woken by odd goings-on in their bedroom. Both of them reported hearing a loud noise, as if someone had dropped to the floor from a great height, landing on their feet. Katie leapt up in panic, convinced someone was in the room, but when she flicked the light switch they were the only ones there.

They went back to bed, falling asleep quickly despite the scare. The next day they set off to go to the beach, but as they left they noticed the security gate was wide open. The gate could only be opened with a key! Perhaps they'd been robbed? They went back inside and checked the whole apartment; nothing was missing.

But it kept happening. Every night there would be the noise, every morning the open gate. When they got back they talked to my nephew. Apparently this was not the first time oddness had been reported at the apartment. Noises, open gates, and in the worst case, the building manager, an ex-pat called Bill pushed down the stairs!

Darren, my nephew, did a little bit of research on the property. He learned that the former owner had hung himself in the bedroom Michael and Katie had been sleeping in. He went on to tell us about another encounter he'd had in a property he'd been renovating to sell. Staying in the house he'd been woken by the sound of a little girl crying at the foot of the bed but his torch had shown the room as empty. Is it a coincidence that these two things happened, both in properties owned by Darren? Or could it be the spirits we'd stirred up at the Bastion have wound their tentacles into the wider world, using my family as a bridge? Are these beings bound by time, or can they reach into the past?

15

Lilith

Because, if not an evil spirit reaching back into the past then what else would explain the evil that invaded our family in the early Seventies? She had come into our lives when she trapped my brother into what was practically a shotgun wedding. Pregnant at fifteen, my brother only sixteen and only weeks from breaking up with his childhood sweetheart, Katie. Katie was a down to earth Londoner, loved by everyone in the family, Lilith was not.

Why hadn't Katie and my brother stayed together? Her father was possessive colouring into controlling and did not approve of my brother. He forced them apart, my brother not being good enough for his daughter, and in doing so opened the door to Lilith.

Lilith was a babysitter for a local family on the estate. They met, one day, outside the house, and that was that. Nothing more than a rebound, Michael should have been with Katie but he became trapped by Lilith. She was fucking evil, a vile creature who invaded our family creating havoc. She enjoyed every moment of the mayhem she wrought, her sadistic pleasure that of a textbook psychopath.

Her lack of empathy served her well as she tortured those around her. She didn't care about anyone else and would use anything at her disposal to get her own way. She would fuck other men, not caring when she was caught. Later the rumour that she'd been caught fucking by her own son stuck to her like the smell of shit on a shoe. I don't know if that was true.

My first glimpse of her inner darkness came when her child was only a few months old and she picked him up by one arm. She dragged him across the room as if he were a doll. She didn't give a shit about him, seeing him as a way to shackle my brother into a life of what was tantamount to slavery. Where she used the child as a shackle, she used my brother as a weapon to wreak her vengeance.

One morning, when I was twelve or thirteen, I woke early. Making my way downstairs, a bowl of Corn Flakes the only thing on my mind, I saw her standing by the front door. As she turned towards me the letter she had just let go of dropped onto the mat, looking for all the world like it had been delivered a moment earlier. She saw me, I saw her. She picked up the letter and stuffed it back into a pocket.

I tried to tell Michael, but he merely thumped me. For why would he believe me? He loathed me thanks to the naked favouritism my Father showed towards him: Dad hated me so Michael also hated me. Michael would tell me I was a grass, a tale teller, a bullshitter. Lilith could do no wrong, even as she tortured him down the years with letters she wrote to him.

This creature had no maternal qualities, was devoid of love, the embodiment of pure evil. I wasn't alone in thinking this - outside of the bubble of grace she lived in with Michael, the family hated her. We prayed for justice.

But those letters! She sent them year in year out, driving Michael to the edge of madness. She got off on mentally torturing my brother and dragged her own children and their children into her web of cruelty. God alone, if He exists, knows how she'll be treated come Judgement Day. Whatever the case, her Earthly judgement took place in early 2018.

Yes, justice came to her, and I can't help but feel it was the result of intervention by the same unseen forces of light that had gathered when my father died. I was sure they'd swirled around him in his final months, driving the blossoming of his cold heart into one of kindness and deep regret. His last request had been that the wounds he'd inflicted on the family be healed.

I'm convinced what happened with Michael and Lilith was the result of some divine intervention. Out of seemingly nowhere a thought came to my brother, a notion creeping past his defences. It was as if a blindfold had been removed and he saw clearly for the first time in forty two years. What he saw he didn't like, what he saw clearly was what he'd shared his life with. In what, at the time, felt like an instant but was actually a slowly growing realisation, he became aware of the myriad wrongs Lilith had done him.

He became aware of the infidelities, the thefts. All her sins became clear to him. He became ill, sicker than he'd ever been and ended up in hospital. While there, he felt one of the nurses seemed familiar but it was only months later when the penny dropped for him - she was an old school friend of Katie. Katie, the childhood sweetheart who'd been so cruelly taken from him, Katie the one true love who had been as loved by the family as himself, Katie the woman who he had always meant to be with.

His resolve now cast, he took to the internet to find her. Social media brought her back to him - he found her, he discovered she was living alone, he reached out to her. The flame of their love reignited and Michael finally worked up the courage to leave Lilith for good.

Lilith did not take it well. She went insane with rage, lashing out, cursing the world and my brother. Karma had clearly not lost Lilith's address, it had in fact been biding its time waiting for the moment to arrive on her doorstep with the justice she so richly deserved. I genuinely believe, even to this day, that justice was heaven sent.

The pieces of the supernatural puzzle came together. Where I had needed to see real demons with my own eyes to have a chance of believing, all my brother had to do was live with one. Just as my eyes were opened by the events I witnessed in the Bastion so Michael's were opened by a spiritual intervention.

But when the shit hit the fan no-one else ran to his assistance, just me. I honoured what my father requested and reached out to heal the pain. As the years have passed that bond, forged in the promise made to my father, has only grown stronger.

But even better, Michael had rediscovered true love. No longer was he with the evil Lilith, the woman who had treated him as nothing more than a mobile cash point. When Lilith realised she lost her shit, spitting venom and spreading lies about her now ex-husband.

Some weeks passed and Michael learned even more about the horrors of being with Lilith. He discovered his bank accounts were gutted, that she'd been forging his signature, and even discussed having him murdered. He learned she'd bedded his brother-in-law back in the Seventies. The revelations came thick and fast, while the demonic spirit had reached back into the past and inhabited Lilith another, a spirit of light, had tumbled backwards to counter that evil. For why should we expect beings untethered by location to be shackled by time? There is no reason to expect anything to act as we'd imagine when it comes to the supernatural.

It would have been to our peril to let our guard down, but let it down we did. We foolishly believed the departure of Lilith meant the departure of her evil spirit. How wrong we were.

Of all of those involved it should have been me who recognised the signs. I am ashamed that I did not. During a Bastion visit in summer 2018, my brother's new partner felt a hand on her shoulder where no hand should be. In that dark damp place she cried out in terror, but was it really recognition? I believe the evil haunting the Bastion knew its kin, was drawn to one of its own as it had once been to me.

On initial inspection, Michael had found true love with a gentle, kind, Jehovah's Witness. He'd purged Lilith from his life and was once again safely in the arms of his boyhood sweetheart, but all was not as it seemed. As time went by her behaviour became ever more erratic. Perhaps what they say is true? When one demon is cast out ten more enter.

Her mood would swing violently from one extreme to another without warning. She would flee dinner parties, sometimes not returning only to be found at home saying she'd needed to lie down. Michael couldn't cope with her behaviour and even moved out of their shared home for a while to stop his own health deteriorating.

This couldn't be true, the rest of the family told ourselves, Katie was far too grounded to be as my brother described her. How to reconcile the charming, polite Katie of our experience with the screaming banshee Michael claimed to endure? He told us how the slightest noise could set her off, even the tapping of his fingers on the kitchen table being enough to push her over the edge.

Her noise intolerance became more pronounced, but only in private. In front of the wider family she remained her usual, polite, well kept self. But at home the story was unrecognisable. Michael painted a picture of a hair trigger paranoid, constantly demanding overseas holidays, money and jewellery. I watched this from the sidelines, aghast at what he was telling me. It unfolded with all the grinding inevitability of a train crash playing out in slow motion. We could only watch, powerless to prevent. Her demands became more and more difficult to meet, soon tipping over into impossible and Michael resembled nothing less than an emotional prisoner.

Still her behaviour around the family didn't match what he was telling us. The disconnect between my brother's borderline unhinged ranting and the polite demeanour of his partner jarred with me. I wondered if he was making it all up - had Lilith done more to him than we'd known? Had her mental torture broken his brain?

Months passed, Michael's bank balance trended ever down. I felt I no longer knew my brother; his behaviour increasingly peculiar. He'd been bad during his time with Lilith, but this was a whole new level of being disconnected from reality. He was tired, his words often slurring with fatigue. When I asked him about a holiday he'd been on he confessed he could barely remember any of it. When he asked to spend a few days kipping on our couch to 'recharge', I became certain something was amiss.

Less than a day later, Katie was at the door, begging to be let in and promising to the moon and back that she loved him, wanted to be with him until they both died of old age, and that she would do anything to be with him. The one thing the family wanted was for her to seek help for what we believed to be serious mental health issues, we were glad when she agreed to. He went home with her, and things went right back to where they had been before.

Or they did until Katie asked my wife, during a phone call, whether she should call an ambulance for my brother. She'd found him unresponsive, in bed, his mouth "...full of pills". It sounded fucking made up! A mouth "...full of pills"? What a crock of shit! But I couldn't take any chances, so my wife and I drove over as quickly as we could, me breaking the speed limit, her on the phone to the emergency services.

Writing about Katie and Lilith is hard. Both women were uncaring, twisted, downright nasty - I feel dirtied as I dwell on them.

When we arrived at the flat, Katie showed no concern for us or her partner. We rushed into the bedroom, finding Michael in the state she'd described him, while she made herself a cup of tea. Upon the arrival of the paramedics she finally snapped into action, no, I'm lying, she didn't - she simply made herself another cup of tea! I couldn't fucking believe it! There was my brother, the man who worshipped her, who would do anything for her, struggling for life with enough Valium and Xanex to kill an elephant sloshing through his system, and there was she, giving not one fuck. She calmly sipped her tea, a sight I kept noticing out the corner of my eye, enraging me more and more. I hated her in that moment.

I glanced at her, and in that instant she grinned. But it wasn't Katie grinning, it was something else, something inhuman. I realised, with a sickening lurch, I had seen that face before. Not

Katie's face, that I had seen many times over the years, no, this was the face I'd seen looking back at me from Lilith. Don't misunderstand, it was not Lilith's face either - this smirking visage, revelling in a job well done, was the evil spirit which had projected itself backwards into our family, all those years ago.

As I recognised it, it recognised me or, more accurately, it recognised that I saw if for what it was. The smirk was erased, replaced with a primal furious hatred. In a blink it was gone, her features rearranging themselves into a mask of calm civility, utterly inappropriate for the situation unfolding in the flat.

I looked at the creature with contempt, then turned my attention back to Michael. He wasn't fucking about, he very obviously wanted to die and was refusing the fluid the paramedics were insisting would help him live. The more he refused the drink the more I begged the medical staff to force it down him. They refused, against their code of conduct and ethics they said, couldn't do anything until he passed out, they said. The demon possessing Katie gazed on, a faint smile playing around its lips.

This woman who had claimed she wanted to die with Michael now stood implacably, willing him to die for her. I suspected she had tortured my brother to the point where suicide seemed the only escape. He was losing everything, had seen his children and grandchildren turned against him by Lilith, and now life held no more light for him. He'd spent forty two years trying to break free of one demon, only to run straight into the arms of another, this one twice as vile.

Darkness was clamped around my brother, crushing him from all sides, denying any chance of escape. But that darkness wasn't limited only to Michael - I had seen the demon in Katie for what it was, it knew me now, I was as much a target as Michael. No, I wasn't yet being attacked, but that time would come. Evil does not like to be caught off guard: the events after my sister had captured the image of the demon at the Bastion on that Hallowe'en so long ago attested to that.

The window in which Michael could be saved was rapidly closing. Soon, it would be too late for him to drink down the slimy black concoction the paramedics insisted would soak up the mix of pills breaking down in his stomach. Alison and I got down on our knees and begged Michael to drink the foul liquid, we tried everything, any angle we could think of to change his mind. What did it was reminding him that his death would destroy our mother. She had suffered enough, we told him, please don't make her suffer more! He relented. With a not inconsiderable effort, he choked down the liquid, encouraged by the four of us ranged around him. Katie stayed back, sipping at her latest cup of tea, disinterest written across her face. Did she know something we didn't? Did she think Michael was now too far gone to be saved?

Whatever she thought, she was wrong. Michael immediately started to rally, the shadows surrounding him withdrawing almost before our eyes. As he returned to us, the demon fled leaving the Katie we had always known and loved behind. She snapped into action, distraught at what was happening to the man she claimed to love. This was the Katie I recognised, the

Katie who'd come along and saved Michael from the lifetime of pain with Lilith. But where had she been when her partner was dying? Where indeed!

As the paramedics put Michael in the back of the ambulance, Katie tried to get in as well. Under any other circumstances this would have been entirely normal and correct, but I knew she was now acting out of little but self-interest. Michael was becoming more coherent as the black liquid he'd swallowed took effect. "She's messing with my head!", he moaned, "all she wants to do is break up then make up"

At the request of the medical team, I climbed aboard the ambulance and sat next to Michael. If I kept talking to him, kept getting him to reply then, hopefully, he wouldn't slip into unconsciousness. He ranted at me, "she's fucking mad, she's a fucking mad woman!" I looked at Katie, standing on the pavement outside, she was smirking again! Then, to my despair, she attempted once again to climb up into the ambulance. By now the crew had seen what she was like and, in no uncertain terms, kicked her out and told her to stay out. As the door closed I caught one last glimpse of her, her face a mask of nothingness, staring straight at me unblinking. The doors slammed shut.

All the way to Margate Hospital, my brother kept up a rambling, borderline insane rant about Katie. He told me she was evil, how she'd controlled practically every part of his life. All I could do was sit and listen as he lifted the lid on what had been going on behind the closed door of their shared home. Once at A&E, I was astounded to see Katie had come along in the car with Alison. I couldn't blame my wife, she hadn't been party to the conversation in the ambulance, didn't know what I knew. I was sickened watching Katie's behaviour, her butter-wouldn't-melt dutiful partner act. For anyone who didn't know the truth she appeared calm and concerned, supportive and stoic in the face of the tragedy of her suicidal partner. She was the model of an empathetic Christian woman.

As the treatment pulled Michael back from the brink of the abyss, something peculiar happened. His previous attitude towards Katie dissolved, the accusations and anger forgotten in a matter of moments. I watched the she-beast Katie turn on the charm, I watched everyone sucked into her lie, I watched but I was not tricked.

She turned to me, her charming smile in full effect, "Dave, be a darling, could you get me a tea from the shop?"

"Of course, want any snacks?"

"No, but thank you for asking!" She flashed that grin at me again.

Alison and I made haste to the little shop. I was shaking with anticipation, I wanted to get my own back on the horror, "I'll get you a tea, oh yeah, I'll get you one nice and steaming hot!" I thought.

We bought drinks for all of us, and began the journey back down the corridors to my brother. As we passed a toilet, I turned to Alison and said "I just have to pop in here for a piss"

"Do you want me to take the tea?" She nodded at the two cups I was holding.

"Nah, I'll be good", I replied, and disappeared into the small bathroom. I locked the door, put the two cups of tea on the top of the cistern, and undid my zip. I stood, pissing, waited until I was almost done then tightened my muscles to stop the flow. I took the tea intended for Katie and relaxed, the stream of hot urine topping up the cup, the liquids mixing. I shouldn't be proud of what I did, I'm a grown man, but I was proud and I still am. Perhaps I'd heard she had a fetish for fluids and thought I'd donate?

Michael was still struggling when we returned, me handing the special tea to his partner. His realisation of the horrors of Katie slipped away like a dream at sunrise. Where he'd been so adamant she was the cause of all his pain, now he settled back into being contented. He went home, went back into the lair of the creature inhabiting his partner. At least the whole family was aware of what was going on now. We all vowed to keep an eye on him. We even had the chance to introduce him to our lodger, a wonderful woman who he immediately clicked with. Sadly, he was too honourable, too loyal and nothing happened. He remained enthralled by the weird magic woven by Katie and could see nothing more.

I tried, I tried so hard to break him away, but the men in my family are stubborn and difficult and we all have to learn the hard way. I'm also a big enough man to admit I had no influence over my older brother. A friend once said to me "Pussy will drag you further than dynamite will blow you", I don't really understand what he was going on about, but he was probably right.

At the tail end of 2018 things came unglued once more, shortly after Katie demanded another holiday. Michael couldn't cope and again wound up on my sofa. He'd bought her the holiday, a £500 TV, and a new dining table set; in turn she'd thrown him out. I couldn't help but wonder at her thinking, surely the holiday had been booked for both of them? And couldn't Michael simply cancel it and get his money back? So much of the story made no sense, but I chalked it up to the demonic insanity possessing her.

Whatever the truth of what had gone on, my brother had been kicked to the kerb. In fact, that's exactly where I found him when I drove round - sat on the kerb, head in hands, arse getting cold and soaked from the wet weather. I knew I had to take him in if I didn't want to witness a repeat of the overdose. I had no doubt he'd be successful if he tried again, just as I had no doubt Katie wouldn't stop until he was in the ground.

I thought I had a secret weapon up my sleeve. I wanted to defeat the awful monster and thought Maria, our lodger might be the chisel to break Michael away from the smothering concrete of Katie. When my brother was back under my roof I knew the time had come. Maria liked him and I reminded him of that fact. She would be good for him, I told Michael, Katie couldn't hold a candle to her.

One detail presented a problem; Michael still needed Katie to act as a witness to a brawl he'd been involved in. He'd got into a tussle, she'd been there - he needed her to vouch for him. No-one imagined that she'd use this in her attempt to deliver the final blow to my brother. She did everything she could to stymy his hopes and worked flat out to destroy the whole family. She would have gladly seen her lover in prison.

All I'd done was look out for my brother while keeping my word to my dead father. The forces of evil and darkness want my blood, and may get it one day. Recently, I was diagnosed with an ascending aortic embolism, a ticking time bomb in my chest - these evil bastards won't stop until they have slain me. They will stand above my corpse and they will piss on me, seeking revenge for the urine I topped up Katie's tea with. Never doubt me when I say evil is a real force. I've seen it and it has seen me. Nothing good has ever come from the ten years I have been trying to make this story public. The enemy is using every weapon it has in its arsenal against me, both spiritual and physical. I am faced with people in the real world who harass me, psychopaths all of them.

They are not like us, they feed on our pain. To the psychopath we are sustenance, we are food. They are parasites, riding along behind the eyes of those we know, of those we may have trusted or even loved. Michael has lived with two of them, both inhabited by the same evil. Once you have identified them, you should run the other way, avoid altogether if you can. Michael eventually freed himself of them… after a fashion. Now he has both on his case, both of them working together to destroy him.

Ultimately, I believe none of us can escape - we are doomed to end up on either the side of Good or the side of Evil. The good will become Angels, the bad, Demons. You may think I'm a crank, perhaps I am but I can only tell you what I have experienced - we are a flock of dumb animals, raised on a farm, poised for something greater. Our world is ruled by psychopaths, demons who have taken the highest seats of power. We will one day join the fight, but on which side? Good or Evil? Angel or Demon? I don't know which I will be.

16

Our Mother

An example of one of the Angelic beings was our mother. Though I remain convinced we all move onto one side or other of the Great War, some display the outward signs of allegiance while still in this world. Mum was one of those people. She was long suffering, ever patient, would forgive anyone. No matter how severe the abuse she might suffer, she never failed to forgive. She welcomed everyone into her home and gave what she had, even when she didn't have much. I remember her buying me a pair of Doc Martens' boots costing most of her wages - she didn't complain, she didn't lord it over me, she just did what she could, acting out of love. Sadly her good nature was often taken advantage of by the cruel, parasitical, and evil.

She would forgive a person even if they robbed her of her very life! As I look back on her, or the memory of her (which is all I have) a dreadful emptiness settles on me. I feel her loss keenly as a crushing ache in my chest. I miss her everyday, my broken heart yearning to speak to her again. I needed her calming voice as things became more and more bizarre in my life. She'd been the anchor to the family boat, holding us in place as the storms of life lashed at us - now we were all adrift, all suffering.

Don't mistake my sorrow for self-pity. Death is inevitable, that Great Wall of existential annihilation waiting for all of us. Everybody dies. No, I feel sorry that her children were too wrapped up in being kids to notice all the sacrifices she made. A million tiny kindnesses, daily settings of her own needs aside. My father was a miser and gave almost nothing to my mother to keep us clothed and fed. We scrambled around for pennies, making every single one count. He lived like a fucking king!

Why did he give nothing to my mother? He earned a fair bob but so little of it made it back to our home we practically lived in poverty. In later years, after his passing, us siblings wondered what he'd done with it all. As far as we knew, he didn't drink or take drugs. Yes, he smoked forty a day, which would cost an eye watering amount now, but this was back in the day when fags were as cheap as a bag of chips.

Did he have a second family? He often stayed out all night, fishing. Was he lying about that? No, it seemed unlikely, as he always returned with fresh fish. He was very close to a couple of local women, a tattooed, aggressive, boiler straight out of a TV prison drama, and a neighbour up the street. The former I remember very little of, the later that he often gave her the fish he caught.

Recently, Michael turned to me and said "Do you think Dad had a secret second family?" It was a good question, was he a serial womaniser, a philanderer? If he was it would explain a whole host of things, not least my own penchant for relationships with women.

This is all besides the point though and draws my thoughts away from my sorrow at the absence of my mother. She deserved more than my shit of a father gave her, whether he was fucking other women or not. It wasn't just her own kids she showed kindness to, any child in need was looked on with love by her. It might sound insane, but in 2017 my sisters went to see a medium in Spain who told her mum's purpose in the spirit realm was to tend to the children and the orphans. This caused me a raised eyebrow: where were the parents of the orphans? Surely they'd have been in the spirit world, waiting for their family to be reunited? Perhaps the kids' mums and dads had been evil and had ended up in Hell! Whatever the cause of the spirit kids separation from their spirit parents, it warmed my heart to know mum was still beavering away, protecting the innocent.

If only she'd been able to enjoy the experience when alive! The poor woman watched helplessly as her children waged open war on one another. How these dark hate filled days must have deeply cut her! She was so full of love and we were so full of hate. For such a frail angelic being this must have been torture to witness and I will feel forever guilty for my part in it. There's not a day passes that I don't speak my sorrow and regret into the void, hoping against hope she can hear me.

My attitude towards the concepts of heaven, hell, and even God are difficult to explain, but if anyone deserved the afterlife paradise of heaven then it is mum. God knows, her suffering was almost constant! Raped at knife point by a prisoner of war, she received no support from her family when she fell pregnant. How despicable! How lacking in empathy my grandmother must have been! She was forced to wear a corset to hide the bump, then sent to a convent when that became impossible. Robin was the result of that unholy union. I draw only the scantest solace that her alleged rapist died alone in a shithole in Oldham - it was better than he deserved.

Mum had very little time with my grandfather. Much older than my grandmother he died when mum was small. He was from Canada, a lumberjack who had travelled via tramp steamer to the UK. God alone knows what he was thinking, swapping the endless forests of North America for the bucolic woods of England! His poor judgment stretched into other parts of his life and he served time in jail for cheque fraud. He said it was to feed his family during the Depression, but was this another attempt at retrospectively justifying a decision?

He was also deeply, terribly, paranoid. He was convinced he was being pursued by someone, being observed by something. He saw phantoms and watching eyes on every corner, behind every door. Was he ill? Or was the evil I'd awoken in the Bastion responsible? Like the vile spirit which had reached back through time to infect our lives via first Lilith and then Katie, had its shadow been cast even further into the past?

Mum's childhood was tough. Her brothers, Ronnie and Ernie took on the role of father in the household. By all accounts Ronnie was a tough old lad in his day but was always a gent.

Those brothers of her's looked after her, looked out for her, and made the years without a father less awful.

My mother is in another book, a novel titled 'Wouldn't Have Missed It For The World' about the history of the Women's Land Army. There is a photo of her in the book, a young woman in a cowboy hat, holding a guitar, part of the entertainment for the Royal Air Force. It was there she met my father, breaking up after a short romance. An aunt intervened, and soon they were back together and living, along with the now adopted Robin, in the married quarters at Stanmore in Middlesex. They lived there, mum bringing up Robin, dad working on Spitfires and Hurricanes, sometimes being posted overseas. Soon Robin was joined by two daughters, Jane and Christine, then Michael, then me.

My father left the Air Force in 1957 and moved the family to an end terrace council house in Canterbury. I still live there. I was born in 1963 and the family was complete. Despite being adopted by dad, Robin was never accepted by him. Worse, he treated him terribly, often beating him so hard the poor lad was sick. Eventually Uncle Ernie intervened and Robin was, for his own protection, placed into care.

As a toddler, I frequently witnessed these psychotic attacks on Robin. I would cower behind the furniture, making myself as small as possible, as my father raged and thundered around the room. Robin was terrified, but his attempts to flee came to nothing as my much bigger father meted out his temper. I wasn't safe for long, soon his attention turned to me, and then my mother as my father talked with anger and fists rather than reason and words.

Michael, conversely, was his Golden Boy, the apple of his eye who could do practically nothing wrong. In fact, I can only remember one time when my father lashed out at his favourite son. Michael had crashed his scooter and came into the house dazed, stumbling, and slurring his words. Dad immediately leapt to action to see if he was ok... no, of course he didn't, he leapt up and punched Michael full in the face 'for being drunk'. He didn't bother to find out the truth before jumping to his conclusion.

Father had no compassion, no empathy. As a child I suffered from horrendous ear infections, the pain so intense I would scream in agony as I lay in bed. Rather than help, dad would bellow up the stairs "For Christ's sake, SHUT UP!" If I continued to cry, he would come up into the room and make mocking sobbing noises.

He was an evil bastard when he was younger as well. Why had he had children at all? He obviously hated them. He was the opposite of my mother, where he was violent she would embrace, his screams of rage would be met by her words of soothing. She was terrified of him, but also defiant towards him. When he mocked me over my ear pain she would bring me downstairs into our cold, unheated front room, fold me in a blanket, and hold a towel-wrapped hot water bottle to my ear. This would alleviate the pain, at least for a while.

Many times I would have blood and pus discharging from my ear. Once, it got so bad the family doctor was called out and he told my parents off for not taking me to the hospital. My temperature was sky high and I was a gnat's whisker from becoming gravely ill. I felt bad that mum had been equally blamed, she had tried her best but dad's lack of concern was the real culprit. He simply couldn't be fucked to get out of bed to take me to the local hospital. Who can blame him? It was a whole three minute drive away!

My evil scumbag of a father stole my childhood from me. I couldn't understand what I'd done to make him so constantly furious with me. I was equally confused by Michael, his violent outbursts seemed driven purely by hatred. I'd been born when he was four, and he resented my very existence. His hatred of me matched that of my father, but I was too young to understand it at the time. How does a tiny child comprehend hate? But hatred clung to me like the smell of damp on a dog which has come in out of the rain.

Hate swirled around me, through me, and followed me all of my days. But now I understand where it came from: just as those grasping shadows of evil had reached back to Lilith, so they groped their way into the deeper past. They sought out cracks in the past, twisted wide any gaps they discovered. And we didn't realise what was causing all this malevolence! How could we? How could we even begin to comprehend that something I hadn't yet done was squeezing my life into a broken twist of wrongness? It is the nature of the non-temporally bound that the effects of one's actions are felt many years before they take place. In this way I understand free will might be an illusion - if I was reaping the results of my 21st Century actions at the Bastion half a century earlier could I have ever avoided that fate? The time shifted effect begat the cause, which then triggered the effect in the past - time is complicated, and evil's manipulation of it doubly so.

But, of course, I was oblivious to this as a child. My brother and I never knew any peace, and my father always took his side. I would flee to the bathroom, the only room in the house with a lock on the door. There I would lie on the floor, my feet against the cistern and my head and shoulders against the door, holding his attempts to batter his way in at bay. Sometimes I wasn't strong enough, sometimes he forced his way in and my raging beast of a brother would make me pay, his fists acting as debt collectors. Other times I held him back, kept him out of the tiny locked room until my father came home. With dad in the house, Michael would calm down, not daring to pummel me in front of a parent. I'd try to tell my father what had happened, "Don't tell tales" would always be his reply. He refused to believe his favourite could ever do such a thing. Saintly Michael, the Golden One! Never could it be suggested the mighty, wonderful, Michael had done anything to me! But he did, he bullied me senseless, and his bullying encouraged the other kids on the estate to torment me as well.

I wish I could say I rose above it, that the constant fear didn't sink its vile teeth into me, but I cannot. I became what I hated, I became the monster I believed both my brother and father to be. As I grew, a loathing for authority gnawed within me. I had lost all my innocence. I saw rules and laws as things to be broken, the more spectacular the nature of that breaking the better. I stole, I fought, nothing held me back. Father lost his grip on me as I learned from him - Might is Right, was the lesson. I ran angry and wild, driving cars and motorbikes on the road at twelve. The police became regular visitors to that end terrace in Canterbury but I would not be told. I saw myself as above the law, as someone who didn't need to pay any attention to the rules.

School was unknown to me, no matter how hard mum and dad tried to get me to go. I would be taken to the front door and be walking out the back minutes later. I smoked, a habit I picked up when I was eight and one of my sisters gave me a fag as we took the train to Faversham Swimming Baths. I was hooked for life. At twelve I discovered girls, losing my virginity to a redhead several years older than me. At thirteen I fucked a forty year old nurse. She was blonde and I loved every moment of it as I ploughed her like a field!

I was running wild, getting wilder with each passing year, but I was still terrified of my brother. The sound of his voice was enough to send an ice water chill right down my spine. He was already palling around with Lilith by then, and her voice soon took on the same Pavlovian power as his. I walked on eggshells, in constant fear of enraging them. He would attack me with fists, she would use lies and deceit - they hurt equally.

Hate became the norm in my family. Morning, noon and night we gorged on a diet of animosity. Behind most of it stood Lilith, the demon possessed monster, another artefact of my future visit to the Bastion. Even my girlfriends weren't safe, she was vile to them, seeing any other female as a direct challenger to her supremacy.

Now, when Michael and I fought (which was often), there was the added dimension of Lilith. Lilith, a malevolent shadow hovering over my brother at all times, ready to pour poison into his ear. It is a wonder we didn't kill each other, Michael and I. God knows we tried, oh how we tried! A tearful mum would look at us and despair, wishing we were like Jonathan and David rather than Cain and Abel. If you'd have told me we'd both still be alive in our fifties, I wouldn't have believed you.

I became more and more twisted, more and more evil. Hatred and bile twisted and turned me into something dark and loathsome. I wished death on Michael and Lilith. I don't mean I idly thought how nice it would be if they were gone, no, I let the fantasy of their violent end consume me. I obsessed over the ways in which they could meet their maker, visualising the most appalling of degradations being poured upon them followed by a painful drawn out death.

They wished the same on me. And so the cycle of hatred spun and bloomed black flowers of evil.

Over all of us was Dad. He did nothing to calm his warring sons, if anything he seemed to enjoy watching us biting at one another. He should never have been a father, he lacked every talent required for the role - in lieu of love and patience he demonstrated rage and mockery. He was cruel, delighting in all things painful and hateful. Even his own mother commented on how lacking in love he was! A short while before she died she told me she believed he was rotten to the core. Like my mum, Gran was an angel amongst us, and almost as patient as her daughter-in-law. For her to say my father was irredeemable was quite something.

But I shared blood with my father, and that evil pumping through his veins pumped also through mine. I had no hope of being a good person with such toxic poison a part of me. Evil wanted me and provided the greatest tutors imaginable in my brother and father.

I adopted the creed of 'get what you can, while you can'; I didn't care who got hurt in the process of this procurement. Rules and law meant nothing to me and I became the model of my father, a selfish violent man. I screwed over everyone I met and I fucked around. I was not the only one, other than Robin and my sisters, my family was a violent brood of vipers more akin to the Manson Family than Partridge. In the centre of this hurricane of rage stood my mother, suffering silently as we tore at each other. My sisters tried to help her, showing the women of our family to be better than us men. Lilith wasn't a blood relative, and she pulled the strings as us men fought. Lilith screwed every swinging dick she could find, paying no heed to the pain she caused Michael. But who am I to judge? I was just as bad, using women for my selfish pleasure, discarding them. As the years rolled around, the number of women I'd fucked my way through only grew. Maybe I can cut myself some slack here, unlike Lilith it wasn't simply about the sex for me, rather the thrill of the chase, the catch, the possible romance. I paid a cost though, I became emotionally attached to many of my conquests, spending a great deal of time in heartbroken dejection when things went tits up.

Yes, love hurts, it snakes its way into every gap and crack, and its withdrawal is agony. I searched for the love I had never experienced from my father, but the procession of pretty young women couldn't fill that role. I can't deny I was addicted to women, though. Being with a woman was the greatest joy I could experience, but it was also the greatest pain. Over the years it became a self-inflicted torture. I apologise now to all the women I used over the years and hope you draw consolation from my subsequent downfall.

Karma came knocking at my door, and in 1981 I woke up one morning in Borstal.

17

Sadly You are in Need of Training. HM Borstal 1981

After getting away with the worst possible behaviour for such a long time, the past finally caught up with me. I had gambled that I was untouchable, that the Police and Crown Prosecution Service couldn't touch me, now I'd lost.

I should have expected it, it wasn't as if I'd genuinely gotten away with everything I'd done - I'd had some close shaves resulting in Community Service Probation, so I was definitely on the radar of the law. The final straw had, most likely, been me riding my finely tuned Suzuki GT 250 to the latest round of community service. I was banned from driving at the time, it's possible I was doing the service for that very reason. The supervisor was furious and disgusted with me and called the police. They failed to catch me, as I rode home via a different route. I laughed at their idiocy! The following week they tried again - yes, despite my close call I had gone back to the community service, once again on my bike! I was either brave, full of youthful cocksuredness, or stupid. I rather suspect it was a mixture of the three.

I finished the day's work, cheekily waved at the supervisor who turned her head away from me in a manner I can only describe as rude, and hopped on my bike. How dare she look at me like that! The disrespectful bitch, I thought, as I raced off towards home. At the edge of the village I saw a Police motorbike. Shit! This was meant to be my safe route, the one I considered unlikely to ever be monitored! I swung my Suzuki around and, as casually as I could, went back the way I'd come. I felt pleased with myself, I'd seen the copper's trap and slipped out of it. I was fucking Fantastic Mister Fox! I was the great Houdini!

As I approached the countryside from another direction I spotted two Policemen standing next to their Rover. Fuck me! They were here as well? I felt a little anxious, but at lest there was one last route I hadn't tried - I doubted they'd block all exits just to catch me! Trying not draw attention, I turned the bike around and, cool as a cucumber, rode off in the opposite direction as if I hadn't a concern in the world. In reality my heart was pounding, what the fuck was going on? As I swung around the bend onto the straight leading to the only remaining exit from the village I saw a Police car and another bike! Jesus fucking Christ! I was fucking screwed!

I had no choice now, I had nowhere else to go. Maybe I was paranoid? Maybe they weren't there for me? Of course, that was it, I was imagining I was more important than I actually was! "You daft fucker, Dave!" I chuckled to myself, "They're not after you at all!" Emboldened by my act of self-convincing, I gunned the bike - I'd pass them at a speed, not so fast they'd do me for going too fast, but enough that they'd know I was taking the piss out of them.

As I roared down the lane, I saw the driver of the car putting his seatbelt back on, and then the biker starting his machine. Coincidence, surely? I sailed past, waving and smiling as I went. I was out! Fan-fucking-tastic! I'd been right, I was paranoid, they weren't after me.

Then I heard the siren. I glanced in my mirror and saw the car and the bike behind me, their blue lights flashing. All I could do now was try to outrun them. Though I vaguely knew there was no escape, that the police knew where I lived, I reckoned I could get away if I was just fast enough. I accelerated. As I passed the turn off for a lane on the right another police bike skidded out of it. God, they weren't messing about! I pushed the bike harder, the engine screaming as I gunned it. Another quick look in the mirror told me I was on a hiding to nothing, the police machines were just better, faster, and ridden by men who knew what to do.

I considered what to do, the hedges flashing by on either side. It was game over, I couldn't outrun them and I didn't know the fields either side so there was no escape there. I flicked my indicator to signal I was stopping and let the revs drop away, a police bike reaching me almost immediately. I stopped, turned off the motor, and waited. I could see the police officer walking towards me in my mirror. I turned to him and smiled, "Afternoon, mate! What can I do for you?"

He looked at me, paused for a moment, then said "You're nicked"

It didn't help that they also wanted me for GBH. A few weeks earlier I'd been paid by a bloke to steal a 250 Honda Super Dream, he wanted it for parts for his own bike. I did the deed, delivered the bike... and the dopey clown began stripping it there and then, in the car park of the station where he worked! It was broad daylight! I couldn't believe what he was doing, and was even more stunned when he grassed me up after being caught! To make matters worse, the bike had belonged to a copper!

A short while before the police finally caught up with me, I caught up with the bloke who'd grassed. As I approached him, calling him all the names under the sun, he pulled a machete on me! A fucking machete! I went for him, reasoning I had to at least get the blade out of his hand. I did but, as it went spinning off over a low wall, he sunk his vile yellow rotten teeth into my arm!

He clamped down, breaking the skin and drawing blood. It was agony and the little rat wouldn't let go. I desperately looked around, the machete was lost but I could see some fence posts nearby. I dragged both of us over to the pile, grabbed one, and set about beating the toe rag about the head and upper body. It was only after the fence post snapped that he let go.

I thought I'd been so clever, such a smart young man. I'd bobbed and weaved, sidestepped the law over and over. I'd thumbed my nose at the Police, believing myself to be untouchable. So when Judge John Streeter said, as I stood before him, "Sadly, boy, you are in need of some training", I was still shocked when he continued, "I sentence you to a term in Borstal, to be no less than six months but not to exceed two years."

I gave up my name and became Prisoner D59832.

18

You're a Stowe Boy Now

I spent two weeks in Canterbury nick, then a week in Rochester. I was awaiting allocation to the centre where I'd spend my sentence. The choice came down to Dover Borstal or Hollesly Bay Colony, near Ipswich. The latter gave the option of working outside, so I was happy to be sent there. I shouldn't have been.

I had thought I might get some fresh air, learn a few things, but all I learned was how to take a beating in a hostile environment. The staff stayed out of it, allowing the other boys to dole out the violence. There was one lad, Bains, a grizzly Essex Monster who I soon learned was the 'Dorm Chap'. This made him the boss, the one who told you what to do. If he told you to jump you didn't even wait to ask how high, you did your best and hoped he wouldn't fuck you up for getting it wrong. I was scared he might kill me.

All this sounds unlikely, doesn't it? But believe me it's how it was. A lot of the boys were on HMP sentences, meaning they were too young to go into the adult prison population but had been banged up for life. These were fucked up individuals, murderers, hopeless cases who knew they would never again taste freedom.

I say all I learned was how to take a beating, but that's not true. I also learned how to take a slashing. Several times I was cut with razors, then beaten unconscious. I suppose you could fold those two into a single lesson, but I prefer to separate them out.

There's no romanticism to be squeezed from the Borstal experience, nothing to be looked back on fondly. I experienced racially charged riots, suicides, escape attempts… all on top of the near daily assaults. The stench of imminent threat was constant, a buzz that hung in the air, cracking like electricity. Yes, I gained some skills in engine rebuilding and repair, respraying, even road testing once I'd been there long enough for the screws to trust me. There was even occasional jam purloined from the on-site jam factory (believe it or not, we made the jam for the whole prison service!) but I cannot deny that I was over the moon when my eight months inside came to an end.

The violence, institutionalised racism, the terrible food - I hated it all. It seems such a long time ago, but some of those memories are as fresh as If they'd happened yesterday.

19

Time for Your Discharge Beating

The Stowe Unit, my home in Borstal for all those weeks, had one final treat in store. A tradition had emerged over the years, a violent tradition. The 'Discharge beating' was ignored by the screws, possibly even secretly encouraged by them. One last turn of the correctional knife before a boy was released! So it was I found myself, on my last hours inside, standing in the dark with a steel chair grasped firmly in my hands. The Borstal was open, meaning we didn't get locked into our cells at night. While this had some benefits it also had considerable downsides, the ease of access by enemies chief amongst them.

I stood in the dark, waiting. The sounds of the unit gradually died down, the cat calls, the shouts of "shut up!" from the night staff. At around 2 am the only sound was snoring and maybe the low groan of a boy having a surreptitious wank. I waited, wide awake, my dark adjusted eyes watching the door. The chorus of snores was suddenly joined by the snick of a door knob being turned, my door knob! The door opened slowly, whoever it was on the other side taking care not to hit the point where it would squeak.

Then a head, impossible to identify in the dark, peered in. I brought the chair down hard, "Fuck you, you fucker!" I shouted, my yell drowned out by the shriek of pain from my wouldbe attacker. He fell back into the corridor, howling. I swiftly put the chair down, kicked the door shut and dived under the covers. My heart pounded as I heard lights snap on in the hall and the approaching footfall of the screws. My door was opened, a guard striding in, "What's going on, Chapman?" I acted bleary, as if woken by this intrusion, "Hmph, what? Er?" I mumbled. The guard looked at me for a long moment, then said, "Never mind, get back to sleep"

I left early the next morning, the victim of my nighttime chair whacking unknown. I'd hit whoever it was hard, the chair possibly causing real damage. Maybe he was in the infirmary right now, head bandaged and the miserable old doctor shaking his head as he looked at the clipboard at the end of his bed. I gave not a single fuck, I was going home! I was driven to Ipswich station, given a ticket to Canterbury, and sent on my way. As the train picked up speed, I looked out the window, relishing the sight of the countryside rolling past. I was free.

At last, I could see my girlfriend whenever I wanted, open a door to the outside world whenever I pleased. It was strange how small mum and dad's house now felt. I'd lived in the huge Borstal unit, surrounded by hundreds of other people and their constant noise. Even at night there had been no silence, but once at home I found myself disconcerted by the quiet .Mum and dad both snored, but compared to the constant rumble caused by hundreds of boys snoring at once the house was a tomb.

I was lucky though, Alison, my girlfriend, hadn't deserted me when I was inside. I'd kept all her letters, still have them now. She even came in to visit me, the other lads hating me for having such a tasty woman. She always brought me nice things to eat and drink, and I'd grin inside as the other boys looked at her with barely hidden lust. I didn't like it so much when they made comments about her after she'd gone, telling me graphically what they'd like to do to her. Thank god that part of my life was over, that door shut behind me.

I had benefited from being inside though; I was now in great shape from all the work I'd had to do, and the compulsory circuit training had hardened me up no end. I knew how to fight and hurt people, a skill I found useful down the decades.

20

Did I Learn My Lesson?

I learned my lesson in Borstal. I learned I should never do dirty work myself if I could find some other chump willing to do it. But that's all I learned. I became, if anything, more and more ruthless and cruel on my release. I had learned to look after number one, and bollocks to anyone who got in my way.

It didn't take long for Michael and I to come to blows. He'd been so used to dominating me physically before I went away that my new found strength took him by surprise. It wasn't just strength though, there was an evil callousness pumping through my veins. The demon that would later take control of both Katie and Lilith, the demon I would unwittingly waken many years into the future, had me in its thrall. Truly the malevolence that resides in the Bastion has great power, unbound by time and space.

It was a car that finally broke the fragile peace between me and Michael, a piece of shit Hillman Imp I'd sold him. He'd been driving around in it, showing off to the local girls when the front suspension had collapsed. He'd been left humiliated and limping home in a knackered car. He was furious with me!

"You fucking cunt!" he bellowed as he climbed out of the tiny car after it creaked to a stop in the street.

I just grinned at him, "Looks like you might have a rust problem there, Micky"

He didn't take this well, not in the slightest! "You fucking cunt!" he repeated, loud enough for the woman across the road to twitch her curtains. He advanced on me, but I stood my ground, smirking.

"You need to sort this!" he spat at me.

"What? Like, literally fix it?" I smiled again, perhaps I'd have a look under the car.

I opened the boot, figuring I could at least get a look at the floor, see if there was a major rust problem, before getting down on the ground. I pulled up the ratty mat and a couple of garden tools he'd stored in there and lo-and-behold there was a fuck tonne of rust. I turned to tell Michael and was momentarily surprised to find his fist smashing into the side of my head!

My bastard of a brother had lamped me one! He'd waited until my guard was down then thrown a right hook! I staggered, all thoughts of fixing his car immediately forgotten. I was only stunned for a moment, and as the stars cleared from my vision they were replaced with a pulsing red mist. I grabbed the first thing I could get my hands on, a garden fork from the boot of the car. My fist firmly wrapped around its handle, I went at him fully intending to stab him in the face.

As my arm swung up, the three pronged weapon aimed straight and true for Michael's face, he put his hands up to protect himself. The fork was unstoppable, digging into his arm, breaking skin, drawing blood. My big brother shrieked with rage and pain, grabbing his bleeding limb. I took my chance, locked my arm around his neck, and held on until he passed out.

I wanted him dead, I'd had enough. All the years of hatred and resentment poured out in one ruinous act of violence. I tightened my grip, I no longer cared if I went straight back inside, I wanted him destroyed, his consciousness wiped from this world forever. The red rage of the Bastion demon held me, pulsed through my arms, throbbed in my vision. I saw nothing but crimson, heard nothing but the wave-crashing ocean of my blood pumping in my ears. I was a murderer, I was always a murderer, I had always been a murderer. I haunted the dark deep of the Bastion, unable to leave, unable to atone for my crimes. I'd seen my chance, had infected the Chapman family, had reached back into their past and royally fucked them up. My fury overtopped the defences of the vessel I inhabited, this useful vehicle allowing my re-entry into the world.

Then I was being pulled away, my roaring screams wrenched away from my goal. There were people there, Dave's wife… no, not yet, his future wife, I corrected myself, one of his friends, that meddling neighbour, Albert. And Michael's future wife was there! Shouting, spitting with rage. I knew her, I recognised that kindred spirit, saw her clearly - another facet of myself! How deliciously right that she should be the one to tear the life out of this vessel, Dave! She came at him with the garden fork, red with the blood of that bastard brother.

For a moment I split my attention... and in that moment I was gone, and I was back. I gasped, taking in the scene before me, the blood, the angry faces, Mick's girlfriend coming at me with the garden fork. I let go, rolling off him. For what felt like forever, we lay side by side, me unsure what had just happened, him regaining his breath. Then he was coming at me! The fucker had recovered and was coming at me, coming at me with that bloody garden fork! It was then Albert, the neighbour, sprung to action. He was a hard as nails old bruiser and he stopped us, there and then. In that moment of intervention we were all ourselves again. No-one died, that day, though I have no doubt the Bastion spirit craved an execution.

21

The Story of Albert's Ghost

Albert saved at least two lives that day. I feel he deserves more than a passing mention in this book, so I will briefly detour from the main path to tell this story.

Albert, his wife Pam, and their son Kevin, lived next door to us, their garden adjacent. Albert was a former railway worker, a hard old boot who had worked for British Rail, and was respected and liked by everyone who knew him. I had a soft spot for him, he reminded me of a kind, neighbourly, Robert Mitchum.

Not long after the death of my father, Albert also left us. I was gutted. As I said, he was a kind man, and I'd never forgotten the way he'd stepped in all those years ago. I owed my life to him, Michael owed his life to him, he was a treasure to our family. He had simple pleasures, beer, ferrets, his favourite local, there are too few Albert's in this world. He hummed the same little tune wherever he went, a circling almost-melody that never resolved but never became tiresome. If you lived on our street you'd hear it, whether it was being hummed on the way to the pub, or la la la'd as he worked on the back garden.

His death was peaceful, the closest you can come to a 'good death' I can imagine. He went out to the pub, humming his little song, met up with his pals and had a fine evening downing pints and telling jokes until closing time. It was the same evening he'd had a thousand times before, with the same people, and the same jokes. When the landlord good-naturedly kicked them out he made his way home, slightly wobbly from the booze. He fumbled his key into the lock, pausing to greet one of the local cats out on its night prowl, and stumbled up the stairs. He stripped down to his vest and pants, slipped into bed next to Pam, and fell asleep.

He never woke.

There had been nothing to indicate impending departure, no health issues nibbling away at the edge of his well-being. So, while his death was sudden it was also unexpected, free of all the months of pain and sadness which had consumed the final weeks of my father's life. A good death, as I said.

A little while after Albert moved on, I was in the workshop in my back garden, working on a Mercury outboard power head. The machine was up on my bench and I was engrossed in my task. I had finished a small job and was moving the motor around to get at the next thing I needed to work on, when I heard a voice humming a little tune.
  "Alright, Albert!" I said, not looking up and not really thinking.

The prickle of wrongness raced up my spine, a cold chill of realisation. How could it be Albert? I was suddenly so distracted I let go of the outboard causing it to tilt the bench with its unbalanced weight, smash through a window and damage some rather valuable components I had lined up on the patio.

I don't know what shook me more, Albert humming or the damned outboard smashing through the glass, though I know which one cost me the most money! I told his family what had happened, but they looked at me as if I were several sandwiches, a pack of crisps, a thermos, and a picnic basket short of a picnic! I still think of Albert, and I firmly believe he inadvertently caused me to break a load of stuff by humming his little tune. I don't resent him for it, it comforts me to know such a good bloke is still around, still going about his business, still never finishing that melody.

22

My Mother's Death

Where Albert's death had been a fitting and peaceful end to a life well lived, my mother's was one of the worst, most traumatising times of my life. It was a ten day nightmare that will stay with me until the moment I join her.

We'd been watching the Queen's Diamond Jubilee concert, broadcast live on the Beeb from Buckingham Palace. She was happily singing along to Tom Jones when Alison and I turned in for the night. It was early, but my lovely wife had to get up at the crack of dawn to go to work the next day. We left mum to watch the rest of the event. Her staying up into the early hours wasn't anything unusual - most evenings she'd be up past the rest of us, watching Ben Hur, Song of Bernadette, El Cid, or the Sound of Music, movies she'd loved all her life and which never failed to bring her joy.

Alison and I were dropping off to sleep when Connor, our son, burst into the room. "Dad, Dad! There's something wrong with Nan!".

I looked at him, bleary from the almost-sleep I'd been on the cusp of, "What are you going on about?", I asked.

"Fucksake, dad! It's Nan, come quickly!", he yelled, heading off to her room. I followed, and what I saw what something I'd hoped never to witness. Mum was slumped half on the floor, half on the bed, unable to speak or move. Her mouth seemed to be attempting to form words, but all that came out were low groans. Her eyes locked on mine, panic clear beneath the confusion. I lifted her onto the bed, propped her up with a pillow, and called 999.

I fucked that up, something so simple! I should have stayed calm, explained the problem, but instead got so impatient that I lost my rag completely and swore at the woman on the line. I cursed my bad temper and redialled, attempting a level voice as the agent on the other end calmly took the details and address and told me an ambulance was on its way.

It took too long for the paramedics to pull up outside in the ambulance. By now it was clear mum had suffered a stroke, and every second counted. Half an hour after I'd called, half an hour of panicked horror from my mum, half an hour of Alison and I trying our best to calm her, that was when they arrived. They were too late. They tried their best, I'll not take that from them, but it was past the point of no return. The stroke had done its damage, the brain injury profound and irreversible.

But it wasn't a stroke. When we arrived at the hospital a young doctor told her she'd had a brain haemorrhage, so massive she was now unaware of what was going on around her. This was bullshit, I argued! No, no, he insisted, she was unable to comprehend her surroundings or situation. The ward sister joined in, backing the doctor up. She too was adamant mum had no awareness, adding she doubted she was even conscious! All the while, mum lay there, one eye open, watching us, clearly understanding on some level what was going on. Mum was always a fighter, always took the side of her children and she did again in that moment. She waved her frail little arm, groaned a frail little groan. We all turned to her. I asked her to raise her arm again on the count of three - she did it!

I turned to the Ward Sister, a victorious look plastered across my face. No, no, no, that proved nothing she said. I looked at her, for some reason focussing on the gold crucifix hanging from a chain around her neck. As a white hot rage shot up me I remember distinctly wondering whether medical staff were supposed to wear things around their necks, surely a strangulation hazard? Isn't it strange, the thoughts we have during moments of extreme stress? As I had with the first 999 call, I lost my temper, shouting and raging. This time I wasn't the only one, all of the family members present were shouting, pleading. Surely there was something they could do? Please help her doctor! We'll sue the hospital if you don't! Every shade of cajoling and abuse tumbled one over the other out of our panicked mouths.

Things were spiralling out of control and I could sense it was all going to go south at any moment. I had a clear vision of myself being manhandled by a couple of orderlies and a security guard, dragged out of the building and thrown into the car park. I couldn't let that happen, but how to calm down? As luck would have it, one of the doctors piped up that we should put mum on a drip, an act that simultaneously seemed to ease her suffering and apply balm to our need for action. She calmed, we calmed, the situation was defused.

We were moved to a cubicle and within forty minutes she'd regained consciousness! We called family members; her brother and his wife from London, children and grandchildren, all were summoned to her bedside. We had no idea how long she'd last. Perhaps she'd recover, but there was no way to be sure so it seemed prudent to gather everyone together to spend time with her. We didn't want to downplay how serious it all was, didn't want to deny the family the chance to say goodbye if this truly was the end.

She lasted for another ten days, drifting away from us then snapping back. We did what we could to keep her clean, to feed her. The staff didn't care, she wasn't a priority, just another old woman taking up a bed, waiting to die. They even left her in her own filth until we did something about it! Their behaviour was shocking, inexcusable. The family stepped up, we took it in turns to sit with her, staying there around the clock.

Though we had no way to know it at the time, her last conscious moment was tinged with the strangeness our family had suffered for so many years. She sat bolt upright, and reached out towards the foot of the bed, looking through me. I asked if there was anything she needed and went to take her hand, she pushed it away, scowling at my intrusion! I looked at where she was staring, in the direction she was so desperately reaching. Nothing. I looked back at her, for a moment her eyes flicked over to mine, locking for an instant, then the sharpness left them and she slowly fell back onto her pillow. She sunk down and down, her consciousness pulled into that dark warm nothingness that is neither living nor death. I could sense her spirit falling away from me, like someone going from room to room in a house they're moving out of. She stopped in each room, tracing her hand over a familiar light switch here, a textured wallpaper there. She felt the carpet beneath her feet, long worn by years of use, the hessian mesh showing through in the most heavily trodden parts of the house. She drifted through the kitchen, the sounds of years of family life echoing off the now empty cupboards and units. She blew out of the back door, down the garden, and was gone.

We stayed with her, keeping her clean as she lay in the coma. Though I knew she'd already left, I couldn't let go of my need to stay with what had been her physical form. Maybe I had a hope she might come back, open her eyes, smile at us and ask to be taken home? It was a forlorn hope, but one I couldn't shake off. That hope was dashed when the doctor came and quietly explained they would need to remove the fluid drip. Her state was now so far gone the liquid was getting into her lungs. The doctor said she would drown if we didn't take this action. I agreed, but only if they would keep her on morphine, ensure she didn't suddenly wake up in pain and terror.

On the ninth day a new nurse approached us and told us to go home and get some rest. She would stay with mum, keep an eye on her overnight, allow us to rest before coming back the next day. She promised she'd call us if anything happened. When we came back the next day, she'd been true to her word.

She'd taken care of mum, even cleaning her with the aloe body wipes my sister had left by the bed. The space no longer smelt of despair and imminent death, instead it was infused with a clean, living, hopeful scent.

It was the 13th of June. We spent the whole day with her, through the night, and into the morning, when Jane arrived to take up the vigil for us. Alison and I went home to shower and change, the aloe smell following us, filling the house. Once tidied up and refreshed we decided to visit my mother's favourite Roman Catholic Church, the one in the city centre. We lit a candle for her, and as I looked up at the cross I whispered to the broken Son of God hanging from it that it would be a kindness to take her, to end her suffering. I looked at the sculpted eyes of the crucified Christ, mine glazed over with tears, and I begged him to allow her release from pain

As we stepped out of the church on that summer morning, Alison's phone rang, it was Jane and mum had died. I felt a mixture of relief and overwhelming sadness as I stood outside the church. The world continued around me, Alison talking to Jane on the phone, people going about their lives without a care. A mum with a buggy crossed the road in front of us, distracted by her phone, a man hurried along the pavement, one of those courier style bags clasped to his chest. A small group of teens walked towards us, laughing and talking too loudly in that way the young do. There was the sounds of cars, of laughter, of traffic lights, of all the hustle and bustle of life being lived. The world continued to turn, the day ticked from one second to the next, and somehow the sun didn't fall from the sky.

23

A Ghostwriter for a Ghost Story, the Pathway Conspiracy, and Back to the Bastion

I began to consider this a tale worth telling. I felt I had uncovered something when I realised how the Bastion Spirit threaded itself through my life. I had seen things, heard things, experienced things that made it clear some kind of afterlife was almost a certainty. I had to get this knowledge out to people! I faced a problem, I couldn't write for shit! No, reader, I'm not being modest; though I can spin a yarn I am sorely lacking when it comes to getting that yarn down on paper. My words tumble out in a rush, sentences running to hundreds of words, falling over each other in my desperation to tell my story. I needed help. When I realised I needed a ghostwriter, I laughed. A ghostwriter to write about ghosts!

I idly wondered whether my lack of formal education had been caused by the same demon who'd ruined everything else down the years, the self same demon I'd invited into my life that fateful night in the Bastion. Could it be the spirit didn't want me to tell the story? The more I thought about it the more I considered this might be the case! Every realisation, every revelation had come along with an event wrapped in pain or violence!

Even when I started making notes and talking to others via the internet about my experiences, a group turned against me! This cabal of bastards, most claiming to be Christians, spread across the world, went out of their way to make my life a misery. It would be tempting to use this book to settle some scores with them. Oh, how sweet that would be! To name names, to go into the details of their misdeeds! How I would love to lay out, for all to see, the crimes committed by the drug dealer from LA, or the man accused of being a nonce by his own cousin! These losers and liars, I would dearly like to put the boot into them here.

But no, those people are not worth the time. They have fed on my negative reactions to their behaviour, they have gorged themselves on my anguish and pain, they would love nothing more to see their names in print, to know they have got so much under my skin that I would use a whole book for petty point scoring! But no! I will not! I will not allow them to live rent-free in my head! Their names are irrelevant, their behaviour nothing but empty trolling. I am ashamed to have taken their bait in the past, but will not do so again.

In 2013 I found a writer who was willing to handle my story. Dave P, keen to write, eager to hear the story, eager to get it out into the world. We started, and almost immediately we came under attack from the afore mentioned losers, trolls, and lunatics. Against my better judgment I must tell some of what they did: they threatened lawsuits, went after my reputation and that of Dave P. One, an especially demented nutter, claimed he'd written the story! That's right, he tried to claim *my* experiences, *my* life, as his own! This was the Pathway Conspiracy, so-called because of the group they were members of.

After months of stressful attacks from this crowd, Dave P and I gave up. The threats of legal action, though entirely without merit and completely vexatious, had us both rattled. Even a bogus claim could drag on for months, the costs mounting up and up. I didn't want Dave P to be out of pocket, I didn't want to be put through the stress of a court case, and Alison didn't want us to lose the house! If it hadn't been for a fuck-up from the man trying to steal my life the story would never have been told. In 2015 he made a mistake, one so terrible all threat from him was nullified. The decks were cleared, so we started again.

Dave P wanted to see the Bastion, to get a better idea of what I'd experienced. I wanted him to really sense the evil that skulked in the dark passages and cavernous spaces. I had no fear that the demon would be interested in him, it was my family it had tormented for decades, it would surely ignore this innocent man only along to document the tale. We travelled up together in 2017.

He hated the place, he was uneasy, distracted. He kept commenting how quiet it was, how there wasn't even the sound of birds or wildlife. I could see how unhappy he was, so instead suggested we go and look at some of the other sites. He was stunned to discover these places existed! He'd lived in Kent his whole life and didn't know about any of them!

As I drove him home at the end of the day he coughed a few times, real deep lung rattlers. "Are you okay?" I asked. He cleared his throat, took a couple of deep breaths, yes, he was okay he said. By the time I dropped him home he seemed to be having trouble with shortness of breath. But the work had started, he typed away, sculpting gold out of the mud of my storytelling.

I was excited! The book was coming together at last! Soon the world would know about all that had happened, about my father, my mother, Lilith, Katie, the battles with my brother. I would show the world the truth of all I'd uncovered, everything about the evil of the Bastion. Most importantly I'd tell everyone the truth of our layered reality, of how some places are porous, and how spirits and demons are not bound by our narrow experience of linear time. That last was the most mind-blowing: to think something in your future might impact your present! It was insane, but it was the only explanation that made sense. Reality is super-weird, and the beings that inhabit the hidden layers don't want us to tell the truth. But we had thwarted their plans, Dave P and I had sidestepped the dangers, and now the words were pouring out onto the page.

I could not have been more wrong! I now bitterly regret bringing Dave P into the story. Why? Because if I had not he would still be alive. Yes, reader, I hold myself responsible for what happened next. Dave P was struck down with cancer.

I killed him, as surely as if I'd done it with my own bare hands!

The disease slowly ate him away, an all-consuming monster that locked its jaws around him and devoured him piece by piece. He became impossible to work with, becoming furiously angry with me. It appeared I wasn't alone in thinking my actions had caused this dismal fortune. His words towards me became more and more vile, his attempts to hurt me increasingly successful. I couldn't bring myself to see him, to face that wrath and hate. His wife recognised he wasn't himself, tried to make me feel better about what had happened, but I felt awful about it. I hope he achieved some peace in his final weeks.

He died in November 2017, and with him all hope of finishing my story.

24

Back to the Bastion, 2018

But it wasn't over, I couldn't give up. In the summer of 2018 I made a couple of trips back to the Bastion. I had an itch I had to scratch, and I knew I'd never rest until the story was told. I wanted to gather some fresh evidence. Alasdair came along on the first visit, it seemed appropriate that he should be there, given he'd been involved right from the start. We switched on our equipment and almost immediately picked up several very clear EVPs on the Go-Pro. We documented cult linked graffiti, saw the same sigils that had adorned the walls a decade earlier. The place never changes! It's clearly still being used for rituals by fools who have no idea what they're messing with.

The second visit was with my wife, my son, Michael, and Katie. I wanted to get more photos, and Katie wanted to see the site for herself. She regretted her decision before even an hour had passed. Exploring a distant part of the labyrinth she encountered more than she ever expected. She had felt a presence near her, heard voices, then a hand had firmly rested on her shoulder. She'd turned and come face to face with a cloaked figure. She later told us how, as she looked into the darkness under the hood, the figure had faded away. She had screamed, we had heard her, we had rushed to her.

She wasn't alone in being freaked out. We'd been picking up weird signals on our VHF radio from the moment we'd entered the site. This should not have been possible, the tunnels are dug down into chalk hills and radio waves should not have penetrated at all. We made the group decision to leave.

As we left we bumped into a family coming the other way. They had two young boys with them and paused a moment to share some of their tales. The adults knew stories going back to the Sixties, stories of white robe-clad fanatics performing rituals on top of the building. There is no denying the malevolent nature of the Bastion site has been known for many years!

As we drove away we were passed by a shady looking guy on a scooter, and then a car full of young lads, all going to the Bastion. I thought of the family with the two boys, of what a strange thing it was to take them to such an evil dark place for an outing. Maybe it's just me, though. Maybe I've become paranoid over the decades and expect to see the worst wherever I look.

Or, maybe, I've recognised the truth and know just how much trouble we are in.

25

Another Chance, Another Ghostwriter

It barely seems plausible now, considering it after the fact, but my second ghostwriter suffered the same fate as my first. Dave P had commented, shortly before his passing that he hoped the same fate didn't befall any successor. He knew there would be one, he could see how driven I was to have the story out in the world.

Richard Wood was that successor. Richard Wood, a lovely kind-hearted Christian man. Richard Wood, someone I could talk to for hours, and who demonstrated an inner warmth I cannot express in words. Richard Wood, dead from cancer soon after turning his wonderful way with words to the telling of this story.

The spirit of the Bastion did not want my story told.

26

The Quest for Knowledge Goes On

But that spirit has been thwarted. I have found a writer, and I will not name him here. I have passed him what I had and he's wrought something new, something unexpected.

I never gave up, not really, even when I felt like I should. In 2013 I stopped, feeling defeated, but only two years later I was back on track. My constantly seeking nature didn't let it drop, didn't let my voice be silenced. Despite the constant attacks from the lunatic cultists, despite their invasions into my private life for nine long and torturous years, the flame of my desire for understanding burned brighter and brighter. I needed to know how these unseeable spirit entities existed, and how we'd managed to capture them on film and audio several times. I have no real answers, and I wish I had completed a proper level of education before heading along this path. But, as I already know, the Bastion demon's rage spread back through time and I am certain my attitude towards school was soured by it.

Could that have been its mistake, though? My lack of schooling resulted in a mind unindoctrinated into the masses' narrative of what is and isn't possible. I was open to anything, and I researched all I could find. Could arcane man have been onto something? Could the stories of demons, imps, goblins, archons, jinns, spirits, ghosts, elementals and more be ancient man recognising the truth of the layers our reality is made up of? I read about everything, from thermodynamics to Aleister Crowley, nothing was off limits in my search for understanding. With the limited intellect of a council house dwelling underachiever I searched out the truth.

This then, was the mistake the Bastion evil made. It created a man who is very good at what he does. From an early age I've tinkered with everything around me, taken things apart to understand how they worked. My dad, the man who had honed his skills on Spitfires, Hurricanes, and Vampires, told me if I'd gone to school I could have had a brilliant career. He saw in me the very thing that drove me on beyond his death, the tenacity driven into me by the years of hardship the Bastion demon had visited upon me and mine. I wish he'd done it when I was growing up though, I wish he'd encouraged me when that encouragement could have made a difference! No, instead he would snap "David, for Christ's Sake SHUT UP!" I asked a million questions and was given the nickname 'ask me a million questions' in our family.

I am still 'ask me a million questions', still that boy who wanted to know. It was during some of the long conversations dad and I had during his final months that he told me how brilliant I could have been. Typical of that old bastard to leave it too late. I have searched, I have absorbed, I have found truth in theology, demonology, science, the Electric Universe theory, even the works of Tesla. All of these areas have a grain of the whole in them. I wish I were even a fraction as intelligent as the writers of the great works. I wish I could sate my overwhelming obsession with knowing the truth of all things.

I can't begin to describe to you how deeply frustrated I truly am. I wish I was better equipped with intellect enough to take on this impossible task that has now taken over my life. I am no longer the materialist I once was and have lost all passion for the things of my youth. Bikes, fast boats, women - none have the hold over me they once did.

Another of my father's favourite answers springs to mind. As a child in the back seat of the car I would ask "Where are we going dad?", he'd turn around, a giant in my eyes, a man who was still a hero to me and say "Oh, just wait and see!"

Maybe this is the crux of it? I didn't want to 'wait and see', I wanted to know now! Do we only find the full truth when we all take that walk through that final doorway into the unknown? As mum made her final tour of the rooms of her life did she see the answers opening up before her? Perhaps we humans are not intended to know the full story?

This has often played on my mind, should I be sharing this with the world or was it just intended for me and my family? Is this why I have faced such ferocious attacks from multiple directions since this weirdness began on the day my father died?

I am troubled deeply by all of this. I cannot imagine that trouble ever being answered in this life. It will linger, always present until my turn to leave this world arrives. That time could be at any moment, I have my own health issues waiting for their chance to wrench me from my loved ones. Will I return, like so many others have? Will I be trapped in the Bastion? Has the demon residing there already claimed me, marked my future?

Of course, the most horrifying thought is something I dare not express, but know I must. The demon of the Bastion is not bound by time or place and that presents me with the most troubling of possibilities. Could the demon of the Bastion be me? Have I spent my life haunted by a future version of myself? Has the evil spirit that controlled my youth, poisoned two of my brother's loves against him, driven all that is evil around me, been me all along? I pray to whatever god is listening that this is not the case.

Satan himself masquerades as an angel of light. It is not surprising, then, if his servants also masquerade as servants of righteousness. Their end will be what their actions deserve. They should be very fearful as this is what gives them away: they lie, cheat, steal, slander and plot. They are nothing but human vessels for the evil spirits our limited vision of reality hide from us. They have tried to silence me for years, both human and spirit adversaries, they have thrown all they can at me to stop me telling my story.

THE QUEST FOR KNOWLEDGE GOES ON

As I type these final words, I can tell you they have failed.

Epilogue

All that follows is written in my own words...

It would be impossible to list the degree of hardship and balls out torment my family and I have had to endure since 2009 when we first decided to try to bring our true story into the public arena and most of them from the most unlikely of directions, ranging from crazed religious fanatic cults, to dangerous drug dealing gangs living in the two houses next to us over three long years taking over the entire formerly sleepy neighbourhood to which my dear wife Alison and I were the only ones that took a stand against in 2015 through to 2017 resulting in the arrests and convictions of the gang leaders to which we all live in fear of the constant threat of reprisals for our public spirited deeds.

the path i walk has been one fraught with danger at every step and turn of the way, death threats! from religious zealots and drug dealers alike. We have and indeed still are suffering regular catastrophes even as I write.

This has only served to strengthen my resolve to finish this work even at the cost of my last drop of blood and on several occasions that almost became the case. Such is the strength of my doggedly steadfast belief that what we all witnessed was indeed real. Many may consider this nothing more than contrived a hoax or an elaborate money making venture to cream off the profits if any? from the weak minded or gullible. You are wrong on all counts.

I have sunk to the depths of total despair frustrated and broken over so many loved ones and close friends lost along with constant personal disasters the most vicious attacks let downs and crushing disappointments even illness, Yet just when I had reached the point of giving up all hope that this story would ever see print and I had finally been defeated. but who in a million years would have believed the man who salvaged this shipwreck that had foundered upon the rocks would be a well known militant atheist loathed by fundamentalist Christians in the big debate community and one of the heavyweights too.

My god there is an exquisite Irony to all this that I cant help but think has some hidden meaning or purpose to which I know he will totally and completely disagree with.

But there are lessons to be learned here I think? That being two human beings poles apart in their thinking and beliefs can come together and the infinitely more intelligent of the two can put aside his own cast Iron convictions and do a damn fine Job even when everything he stands for tells him this subject matter goes against the very fabric he's cut from.

This is testament to his professionalism as a ghosting agent and I am greatly indebted to him as I had lost all hope that this would ever become a reality he's not such a bad old bearded stick after all.

Dedications

My Mother Betty Chapman (life long devout Christian)

My Father Bernard Chapman

My Brother Robin Dutton

My uncles Ernest and Ronnie Dutton

My Dearly missed friends, Reverend Diane Johnson who's earthly remains were cheekily scattered in the garden of Getsemani. Good for you Diane . Richard Wood also life long devout Christian. Malcolm J ex Radio Caroline DJ

Special Thanks

Special thanks to all those deplorable people that have and still are making every attempt possible to destroy me and this story in the name of Jesus who as you read this sharpen their daggers ready to strike that fatal blow.

Yes I have learned a great deal from them too. The main lesson being I do not need an ancient collection of books written long after events by author's unknown to know that there is a great power behind all things. I simply needed to look right around me with new eyes.

I see the love of a creator built into almost everything i see in the world everyday. The struggles of a mother or father to provide unselfishly for their children when up against overwhelming odds and constant hardship without any hope of reward. I see the love of our creator in every good deed done in secret. Every kind word spoken.

But the same is true of the forces of Evil and how much of that I have done and known in my life. i made the choice not long after these strange events begun all those years ago and it was not by chance to no longer be that man I once was as did my father in his final years.

I see all these mysterious events as a final gift from a remorseful father whom maybe by some odd mysterious unseen force was able to witness the outpouring of love from his children that he threw away almost all of his life at his own funeral.

Childish delusional insane? Not to me or my family and friends who also witnessed the same things.

Only now do I see how truly blessed I indeed am when I look into the loving eyes of my long suffering soulmate lover and wife who has stuck by me since the first time our eyes met on my sixteenth birthday in 1979. Alison, she too is so much like my dear mother. her kind are indeed rare, She has been and always will be my greatest blessing and it took me so long to realize it. I owe everything to her and all that I am and own is hers.

"The Kingdom of God Is Within You" also Hebrews 13:2 springs to mind.

I have no clue how these events happened or the mechanism of which delivered them.

But message received and understood, and indeed with fear and trembling!

I do not reject all man made religions nor do I claim them as my own, I carry no banner I preach to no one if your religion gives you comfort then more power to you. But if it compels you to harm anyone then I have no time for you.

My hope is that this story may provide a glimmer of hope to those who are in need of it and nothing more.

Finally some words of wisdom from my dear friend who performed my wedding not too many years ago.

Laughter and Joy are gifts from god, yet if that laughter is at the expense of another living soul then it was surely forged in the fires of hell itself.
  The Good Reverend Lionel Fanthorpe

David J Chapman, Canterbury, October 2019

Further information

For further information, photographs, and anything else that couldn't be fitted in the book, please visit http://www.thepathwayconspiracy.co.uk

About the Author

David J Chapman was raised in a working class family. The youngest of five siblings he grew up on a council estate, proudly playing in the gutter. He is a devoted husband and father.

He was a staunch atheist until 2009 but is not so sure now. A professional disc jockey and entertainer for over 30 years, he is now retired. Working with many well known acts, he considers those years to be the best of his life.

David became a biker at the age of six when he rode a stolen Suzuki 80. It remains a lifelong passion to this day. He is a lover of all things 'fast n sexy' - boats, cars, women, and bikes he is a self taught mechanic, welder, paintsprayer and engineer, specialising in Outboard Motors. He is also a BSAC Dive Leader and Wreck Diver.

Described by his late friend Richard Wood as a 'wide boy', David has never denied his past as a rogue, thug, womaniser, and petty criminal who spent time in Borstal. In many ways he is typical of those raised in the Sixties and Seventies.

Always inquisitive from childhood, he tells it as he sees it. What you see is what you get.

'The Darkest Path' is his first book.

You can connect with me on:
🌐 http://www.thepathwayconspiracy.co.uk